Frank Stephen Granger

The Worship of the Romans

Frank Stephen Granger

The Worship of the Romans

ISBN/EAN: 9783337007423

Printed in Europe, USA, Canada, Australia, Japan

Cover: Foto ©ninafisch / pixelio.de

More available books at **www.hansebooks.com**

THE
WORSHIP OF THE ROMANS

VIEWED IN RELATION TO THE
ROMAN TEMPERAMENT

BY

FRANK GRANGER, D.Lit.

PROFESSOR IN UNIVERSITY COLLEGE, NOTTINGHAM

"Heaven, hell, the world are within us.   Man is the great abyss."
AMIEL.

METHUEN & CO.
36, ESSEX STREET, STRAND
LONDON
1895

PREFACE

I HAVE attempted in the pages that follow to delineate that group of beliefs which stood in close connection with Roman religion; to point out the manner in which they are related one to another, and to justify them as a necessary factor in the awakening of the religious sentiment. The first chapter traces out the mode in which they are fitted into the organic structure of mental life, viewed as common to a whole nation. The topic of dreams and apparitions suggests that this community of experience extends to all mankind, and, in particular, to the age in which we live. The characteristic beliefs are then traced which the Romans held with respect to the soul, and life after death. After taking account of the manner in which the Romans interpreted their physical surroundings, and especially the miraculous occurrences which formed part of their experience, as the experience of every other people, ancient and modern, we are in a position to understand their worship of Nature. Through watching the Roman mind at work, the observer comes to discern the principles of its operation, and to understand somewhat the practical application of those principles in magic. As magic fades away it passes into divination and prophecy. Having surveyed in this manner the soil in which the later Roman religion grew, we can follow, at a distance, its progress until it loses itself in the purer regions of Greek speculation, and dies before the approach of the Christian faith. The notions of holiness and sacrifice are capable of profound meanings, even amid a religious environment so dreary as that of Rome.

In the treatment of this subject I have allowed myself two liberties, which, to some, may seem to have been abused. I have dwelt, in preference, on obvious and accessible facts, rather than on inferences which rest on acute combinations of authorities.

In the second place, I have availed myself freely of the many modern parallels which present themselves to almost every ancient custom and belief. The melancholy story of the witch-burning at Clonmel, in this very year, gives point to the chapter on magic. Not so long ago a Cornish witch was subjected to persecution by her neighbours in such a way, that the parties made their appearance in the local police-court. There is less difference than pride allows us to admit, between the mind of the early Roman and of the modern Englishman. Some may criticise the freedom with which the usages and ideas of the Christian world have been brought forward to illustrate pagan religion. But there are venerable precedents for dwelling upon the continuity of the religious experience. Christianity was not preached by its first missionary as an isolated phenomenon.[1] I have ventured even to suggest that, in some particulars, current religious observances are less satisfying to the whole nature of man than ancient.

The investigations of folk-lore are really laying the foundations of comparative psychology, on the lines indicated by Mill in his *Logic of the Moral Sciences*. The term suggested by him, Ethology, has never obtained currency. It represents, however, the scope of much contemporary work. The methods of folk-lore are based in the last resort upon those of psychology, and only gain can result from the solution of the problems of the one science in the light of the results of the other. I have tried, in the first chapter, to indicate some of the leading features of the Roman temperament.

It does not seem unreasonable to expect that the student of Latin literature would profit by a

[1] *Acts*, xvii. 22.

somewhat more systematic acquaintance with Roman folk-lore than is customary. The passages quoted and translated in the following pages refer to those aspects of Roman life to which modern life presents few immediate analogies; nevertheless, they often contain the clue to the sense of their context. We can enter into the patriotism, the worldly wisdom, the law-abiding temper, of Cato, Horace, or Livy. We feel strange in the presence of the Flamen Dialis, the augur, or the wolves of the sun-god.

Moreover, this very aspect of Latin studies give them a peculiar fitness to enter into an English curriculum. Each Englishman has some responsibility for the good government of an empire, the inhabitants of which differ from us much in the same degree as the ancient Romans. Sir Alfred Lyall has said that to visit India is like a return to the Roman world.

Let the reader whose memory retains any vestiges of Roman history, try to figure to himself a tribunate exercised in the Rome of Cato by half-a-dozen philanthropists of the present day, who understood neither a word of Latin, nor a fact of Roman history, and he will be able to estimate the likelihood of success which attends the transplanting of English ideas to Indian soil, by persons entirely unacquainted with life in India.

The references which are given at the foot of each page will indicate the writers to whom my obligations are specially great. In particular, I have taken many hints from Mr. Jevons' preface to Plutarch's *Roman Questions*, and from Robertson Smith's *Religion of the Semites*. Mr. G. H. Skipwith has helped me with his advice and criticism in relation to numerous topics, and I have been glad to draw upon his wide reading both for confirmation and disproof.

Nottingham, *Easter*, 1895.

CONTENTS

		PAGE
THE ROMAN SPIRIT		13
DREAMS AND APPARITIONS		28
THE SOUL AND ITS COMPANIONS		53
THE WORLD AROUND		74
NATURE WORSHIP		92
PRIMITIVE THOUGHT		129
ROMAN MAGIC		153
DIVINATION AND PROPHECY		173
THE PRIMITIVE IDEA OF HOLINESS		200
HOLY PLACES AND IDOLATRY		220
THE DIVINE VICTIM		245
THE SACRED DRAMA		269
LATIN INDEX		309
ENGLISH INDEX		311

THE ROMAN SPIRIT

THERE is in the Louvre a large bust of Pentelic marble which portrays the goddess *Roma*, the spirit of Rome. When the rising power of the city began to promise peace to the storm-beaten and weary communities who dwelt on the shores of the Great Sea, they built temples, and celebrated festivals, in honour of their protector, and worshipped her under forms of which the Louvre bust may be taken as representative. The temple which Hadrian consecrated to the goddesses Venus and Rome, marks the rise of a like worship within the walls of the imperial city herself. *Roma aeterna*, Rome the everlasting; such was the name conferred on the goddess, as though the citizens had a presentiment of the decline of the western empire and its capital, and sought by this name to ward it off.

The portrayal of ideas in the form of human beings was very common in both Greek and Roman art. Yet the most enthusiastic students of the antique have shrunk from claiming for this method a universal application. It has been treated as a special characteristic of the Greek genius; an instinct which gives human shape and soul to all objects of the sensible and intellectual worlds. But if it be admitted that we may justly speak of the spirit of Rome, it is difficult to see how an artist could express this spirit more nobly than by a personification of the kind that we are considering. It might even be advanced that we are dealing here with a most natural outcome of the principles of classical art; the various parts of a complex idea are brought together into an organic whole, for this is what we mean by spirit, and receive thereupon a suitable embodiment.

How readily the Greek or Roman mind seized the salient features of social life, becomes clear as we turn to the interpretation of the genius of Athens, which the historian has put into the mouth of her leading statesman; or to the verses with which Anchises in the under world ends the roll-call of the heroic sons of the city. The rendering of Dryden has caught something at least of the rhetoric of the Roman poet.

> " Let others better mould the running mass
>   Of metals, and inform the breathing brass,
>   And soften into flesh a marble face :
>   Plead better at the bar : describe the skies,
>   And when the stars descend, and when they rise.
>   But, Rome, 't is thine alone with awful sway
>   To rule mankind, and make the world obey,
>   Disposing peace and war thy own majestic way.
>   To tame the proud, the fettered slave to free,
>   These are imperial arts, and worthy thee."

It is as though the poet gathered into one ray the varied lights which illumine the names of a Fabius, a Cato, or a Decius; his description setting forth at once the type and the ideal of Roman character. It appears, then, that we are following the clues which sculpture and poetry afford, when we attempt to delineate systematically some of the main currents of Roman thought. Perhaps the reader may protest against the contrast between the ideal of the artist and the poet, and the more sober description contained in the following pages. Yet we must be content to allow for the patriotic exaggeration of a national epic poem, and the sublimity with which adoration invests its objects. A survey of the facts will leave us in a more sympathetic temper than perhaps we anticipate.

There is a scientific sense in which we may speak of the soul of the Roman race. It may be defined as that organized group of beliefs and habits which answered to the conditions of its political life. The human personality is not so much a single existence as a bundle of existences; it might be compared to a small Republic, say one of the South American States, which was constantly changing its president. It will be enough for our present purpose if we take it to be subdivided into the material self, that which is related to our own bodies and material surroundings; the social self, through which we enter into social and political life; and, thirdly, the spiritual self, through which we are conscious of ourselves as persons. We are dealing in this chapter with the second of the three; the social self.[1]

Although the social self, or national character, stands always in very close connection with the physical characters of a race, yet this connection is not invariable. Within certain limits it is possible for men of the most diverse origin to acquire the spirit of one and the same civilization. No more striking example of this could be found than is afforded by the history of Rome. She set her own stamp on nearly all the peoples that came under her sway, and in a manner so effectual that we cease to distinguish the true-born citizen from the foreigner. It is difficult to realise, for instance, that Seneca, the great minister, who was also a philosopher; Lucan, "by his death approved"; and Trajan, the emperor who pushed the boundaries of the Roman dominion to their furthest—were all of them Spaniards. It appears then that this social self is capable of being communicated to a very high degree. When the apostle speaks of putting on "the new man," he is applying to spiritual things a figure illustrated abundantly in the social changes of his time.

The use of the word "person" in Roman law shows that the Romans were conscious themselves of the distinction which holds between the various

---

[1] James, *Textbook of Psychology*, 177.

aspects of the individual life.[1] The term does not always mean a human being; in its original sense it denoted the mask worn, and the part played, by an actor. Then it came to mean the character which each man sustains in the world. Thus a man may be a citizen, a father, a soldier, and so forth. The name person can be applied to each of these conditions with which he is invested. Hence it may be said, *unus homo sustinet plures personas*, a single man sustains several persons. Of all these persons, the most important in the eyes of the Roman legislators was that of citizenship; the condition of citizen including within itself many subordinate persons. If, however, we define it as that person or character which is shared by the members of a political society, we shall see that Roman law merely views from the side of law the same fact as that which we are investigating from the side of psychology. And the admission of foreigners to the Roman franchise was the legal recognition of their acquisition of the Roman character.

The process by which the child tends to put on the character of his elders, is perhaps the most complete example of the manner in which a " person " can be assumed. If we trace what takes place in this very obvious process, we shall be able to imagine the general changes which are effected when an outside people is brought into contact with a long-

---

[1] Austin, *Jurisprudence*, lect. xii.

established civilisation.   Just as the child, in learning to speak, learns also to think very much as those who teach him, so it is with the foreigner.   The Latin language was also the vehicle of Roman ideas, and through the one the foreigner came into contact with the other.   It would be difficult to set this influence of the spoken word too high.   Just as it is the expression of a thought in the breast of the speaker, so it arouses a resembling thought in the hearer, and this process, oftentimes repeated, conveys, so to speak, the soul of one into the other.   This effect of language is well brought out by Dr. Venn : " In regard to any particular society as a whole, it plays a large part in compelling each of us to see the world as his fellows see it."   In some such terms as these we may present the acquisition of a foreign tongue, especially when, as was the case with Rome, there were conveyed modes of thought which far transcended those of most of her neighbours.   If it be true, as Goethe has said, that a man has as many souls as he knows languages, we may at least admit that the change of language means a change of soul.

There is some justification, therefore, for those who would estimate racial descent by the test of speech. The inhabitants of southern Europe may be unable to trace their physical descent from the Romans, but they have inherited their modes of thought and even of feeling.

If language is the instinctive expression of national spirit, law in its positive forms may be viewed as an instrument used, with more or less conscious purpose, to produce a certain type of character. It is of course true that we may not ascribe the whole body of law to such a source. Rules and ordinances, in themselves unreasonable or unmeaning, are retained by prescription and the use of centuries. Nevertheless it is possible in many leading instances to refer the general tendency of positive law to the effort to realise some proposed type of character. This applies not only to the legislation of the Pentateuch and to the Roman code, influenced as it was by Stoic philosophy ; we can trace, though with less certainty, the gropings after ideals of national character, which determine in England our alternating spasms of Conservative and Liberal legislation. Our English law, with its cumbersomeness and want of system, is also marked by a fairness and practical turn, and so reflects, not inaccurately, our national character ; with its desire to get something done even at the sacrifice of that system and method which is in-dispensable to expedition in the long run. And existence under English law, and under the just administration which is the true glory of that law, is guided more or less into the historic moulds of English life. Yet English rule seems to leave traces less deep than those which the Romans have left. In fact, it would almost seem that there was something peculiarly assimilative in the Roman administration, by which it was enabled to render its subjects conformable to the Roman mind. As the English mind speaks through law and administration, so the Roman spoke in tones still more audible through the praetor's edict and the provincial assizes of the empire ; the peace of Rome, which spread round the Mediterranean, was not only external, it rested on an inward community of thought and feeling, which also it helped to produce. This analogy has a practical interest for us. "The provincial administration, as well as the foreign policy of the Roman empire, are reproduced in several notable respects, by our system of government in India."[1] Will English administration create a corresponding change of temperament ?

If it be admitted that language and law are the vehicles of national temperament, by which it is communicated to a greater or less extent to outsiders, the same will be true in a far greater degree of religion. In most ancient communities but little scope was left to the initiative of the individual, at least in comparison with our western liberty ; at every step he was guided by prescription. Whatever he said or did was determined, as to its form at least, by some rule which generally sheltered itself under the name of religion. At Rome, the custom of the elders gathered together all that there was of

---

[1] Lyall, *Asiatic Studies*, pref.

authority and sanctity. Not only the ordinances of worship, therefore, but all customs of speech, belief, and practice, were followed with a sense of their binding force or *religio*. There is no need to dwell upon what is so well accepted, as the derivation of ancient codes from religious sources. There are numerous traces, however, of a like origin in the case of language. Words are divine, magical. The old Egyptians regarded the *true voice*—word and melody taken together—as the gift of the ibis god. "Speak good words," was the injunction with which every Greek ceremony was begun. The Greek mysteries might be celebrated before those alone who were of the sacred tongue. Whatever view of the origin of language be accepted ultimately, it will, in all likelihood, be referred to some social occasion in which the community participates. The tempting suggestion has been made, that language took its rise in "festal excitement," and especially in the war dance. From this standpoint we can understand how it continued to be associated with all the common practices of the tribe, as something upon which the common life depended, and therefore, as will be explained later, as something holy.[1]

Since, therefore, religion in the ancient world comprised every social function, of which law and speech are but two examples, we can see how initiation into the national religion and admittance

[1] Donovan, *Mind*, xvi. 498.

to citizenship went together. The religion of a people was in literal truth the door to its life. The man who was excluded from the practices of the one could not enter into the spirit of the other. And conversely, the frequence, the impressiveness, the delight of ancient ceremonies, were tuning constantly the minds of their devotees to a deep sympathy; a sympathy into which a foreigner could enter but imperfectly.

The most striking and important event in the history of Rome—the breaking down of the exclusiveness of its religion, and the consequent admission of strangers to the national life—is thus of a more complex character than appears at first sight. We have observed this fact in a manner merely superficial, when we have enumerated the legal steps by which citizenship could be acquired. Something more is needed if we are to grasp it fully. We must also take account of the change of temperament which accompanied the spread of Roman law and government round the shores of the Mediterranean.

II.

In a progressive society the ideas of the government represent very imperfectly the average opinion of the governed; for government tends to be exercised—if not directly, at least indirectly—by small bodies of men united by obedience to some group of ideas. And so progress consists very often in the forward march of an active minority, with the great mass of mankind lumbering after them, and now and then getting out of breath. It happens usually, under these circumstances, that the literature and art of an age are rather the product of the governing minority, than the expression of the national life as a whole. The historians, the philosophers, the poets, stand indeed in a very close relation to their immediate surroundings. But this is not all. They are also heralds and guides of the new order of things. The most brilliant periods of the world's history have been those in which the contrast between the government and the governed has reached an acute stage. The circles of Pericles, of the more enlightened Italian princes in the early renaissance, of Elizabeth, acted largely in defiance of the peoples whose resources they wielded. The great writers are, therefore, only imperfect guides to the thoughts and feelings of their contemporaries. If we wish to understand the latter we must have recourse to less direct testimonies; those, in fact, which are included under the name folk-lore. We may mark off, therefore, two layers of mental life; that of the more speculative few, and, on the other hand, the great assemblage of beliefs and expectations which forms the common heritage of a nation.

Histories of literature, of scientific advance, of philosophy, help us to understand the former. It will be the object of the succeeding pages to enter into the latter; to interpret, as far as may be, some of those thoughts which lay nearer to the average Roman mind than the Greek elements in its literature. The great names of Roman literature are, in the main, those of men who belonged to the aristocratic opposition of the end of the Republic, or were under the protection of Augustus and his ministers. Many qualifications must be made before we can take them as the spokesmen of the Roman people. In every one of them, except, perhaps, in Ovid and Tibullus, we can trace a feeling, critical and almost hostile, in regard to their contemporaries. While, however, Lucretius and Cicero seem at times to exaggerate their disagreement with popular beliefs, the case is otherwise with Virgil in his *Aeneid*, and Horace in his later odes. The two great poets of the Empire make great efforts to gather up the threads of the beliefs that still survived, and to weave them into a poetic vestment for the national spirit; not, perhaps, for that spirit as it breathed at the moment, but for the ideal that Augustus and his ministers had formed of it. "The art of moral government," Amiel says, "is to enter into the poesy of an age and guide it." This then was the secret of Augustus' success; he reconciled the demands of a great imperial organisation with the feelings of his subjects. The Empire was, in some measure, more conformable to the national sentiment than the Republic which it replaced. Among other indications of this, it is noteworthy that Augustus favoured the more conservative school of lawyers, in the spirit in which Virgil and Horace found their social ideals in the past. This was a precaution, perhaps, against the abuse of a great extension which he gave to the privileges of the Roman jurisconsults; the knowledge of the principles of law gave the right to deduce and to apply its consequences. Thus, in law as well as in literature, he sought to mould the temperament of his subjects into harmony with the constitution of the state.

This important part of the art of government is left to chance in our time. The inquiry is seldom made whether any given reform is adapted to the intellectual and moral state of those who will be affected by it. What is more surprising still, no adequate use is made of the means provided by the national system of elementary education, in order to make the operation of new reforms as easy as possible.

Much might be done in this way to lighten the weight of social conditions upon the less fortunate classes. Unfortunately, this is the only instrument available. The chaos in which secondary instruction still moves, renders unprofitable any attempt to calculate its effects. Nor is the English law comparable for one moment to the noble instrument which Augustus found to hand in the law of Rome.

We are proud of that practical temper which enables us as a nation to be engaged always on something that wants doing. Yet we fail to give the national spirit a fair outlet and means of expression. Our literature shows the latent powers, which only await the magician's touch to burst forth into action.

But as a nation we seem, somehow, to lack the tact, the knowledge of the art of life, and therefore the happiness which should be ours, and is enjoyed by nations less favoured with this world's goods. Our social life is ungraceful. Our great cities are more solidly built and more wholesome to live in than most foreign cities, yet their effect is mean, and unworthy of the civic life which surges in them. Our public ceremonies are ungainly; and burlesque, oftentimes, the occasions on which they are held.

It is not a mere affectation, then, when many look back with longing to the brilliance of the age of Elizabeth. Then the nation had not yet undertaken the mighty tasks which now it has to carry through. It was not yet distracted by the diversity of its interests. The time seems again to have come, however, when we may look round and ask ourselves whether we should not seek once more that rounded perfection of national life, which is really at our beck and call, had we the patience and self-command, the quietness and confidence, of which we boast ourselves. If the Roman nation, with its many deficiencies, its poor imagination, its crude tastes, its incapacity for abstract thought, attained, to some degree, splendour and fulness of civic life, we ought to be filled with dissatisfaction until, in like manner, our own mode of existence gives full expression to the Anglo-Saxon temperament.

DREAMS AND APPARITIONS

THERE is reason to believe that the effect of modern civilised life upon dream experiences is to weaken them. We have so much to do with printed matter, that instead of remembering things we remember their printed names. Mr. Andrew Lang tells us that he thinks in words, not pictures. We might invert this for the early Roman, and say, with probability, that he thought in pictures, not in words. Further, the complexity of modern experience compels us to think of many things symbolically. For otherwise our minds could not contain what we wished them to hold. Again, the variety of the interests of those who live in populous centres, or who are in touch with them, prevents the current of life wearing deep any single channel. On the other hand, where the sphere of experience is limited, ideas are fewer. Hence, in these cases, the range of dream experiences is limited. Where there is a uniform manner of life, the dream world is often a very close copy of the waking one. If yesterday was like the day before, and is going to be repeated in a thousand to-morrows, the dreams which echo the life of the past will presage, with fair accuracy, the life of the days to come. Add to all this that the primitive mind distinguishes with difficulty between what is true and what is imagined, and we can understand why the dream existence is often placed on a level with that of waking hours.

Again, it is very doubtful whether the undisciplined mind ever attains any really abstract modes of thought. Hence, in the moments when, his more pressing needs being satisfied, such a one can give himself up to contemplation, his state is one of dreaming, of *reverie* in the strict sense. And the panorama that unfolds itself before him in these instants, is almost continuous with the panorama of his dreams. And so the figures which haunted the sleep of the Roman often had their counterparts in the apparitions of the day.

It will have occurred to the reader, perhaps, that the change from ancient to modern life has not been one of unmixed good in this respect. Mr. Lang, like other moderns, would doubtless be content to exchange some of his varied learning for the simpler and more vivid picture thoughts, say of an old Greek. And although the Roman stands on a far lower level in this respect than his eastern neighbour, the difference that separates his mode of thought from ours is still of the same kind. The ancients had the secret of combining vivid imagination with a wide intellectual outlook. We may perhaps be wiser than they, but our modern life seems thin and poor sometimes by the side of theirs. *For every thing we are out of tune—it moves us not.* We have lost the idea of a harmonious upbringing, by which every faculty shall be blended into one concordant being. There may come another age in which this ancient art shall again be practised. And we may find consolation in the thought, that the attempts which are made now-a-days to develop this or that side of humanity may be resolved, discordant as they are, into a new and perfect music.

We ought then to moderate the pride with which our intellectual advance is spoken of. It is one sided. It is not accompanied, for instance, by an answering advance in the perception of what is beautiful. Our English standards of art, so far as the public taste is concerned, are vulgarian and barbarous. We have no more right, however, to claim as our own the finest methods of contemporary science than the highest reaches of contemporary art. Just as no discriminating observer would explain the art of Mr. G. F. Watts, or of Dante Rossetti, by reference to the taste, say, of those who purchased their works, so we have not the right to measure the public mind in respect to science, by reference to the analytical genius of Lord Kelvin, or the dialectical skill of Professor Huxley. True it is, that the terms used in scientific exposition pass into common currency, and in this way the public gets its thinking done by proxy. Yet no one would venture to say that the attitude of the public mind to its duties shows the insight which we might have expected even from this. Let us then be quite candid in drawing the comparison between Roman and English popular thought. Let us admit at once that the Roman was not in truth so benighted intellectually as we might think.

More than this! There is, as we shall have occasion to see, a kind of consistency in the view of the world which we are studying. For one whose mind thinks in pictures, dreams furnish an approach to abstract thought. Perhaps it might even be maintained that they furnish the only occasion on which for such a one abstract thinking is possible. In waking hours the primitive mind is carried away by the changing stream of sense impressions. In sleep, his thoughts, if we may call them so, appear without this factor. Even the writers through whom we become acquainted with Roman antiquity, exhibit side by side with their higher endowments many of the characteristics which have been roughly indicated. We come to know the ancient Roman no less through the indirect indications which these writers give us of their own feelings, than through the positive accounts of popular beliefs and practices.

The figures that appeared to the Roman in the night came singly rather than in companies, and in surroundings of a simple character. The statue, standing lonely and tall and pale, represents, not inaptly, the phantoms that visited him. So it was that Drusus Nero appeared to Pliny the Elder in Germany, and standing by him as he slept, besought that learned man to preserve from oblivion the reputation of the conqueror of Germany. Whereupon Pliny set about writing a history of the German wars in twenty books. The spirits who came to the Romans in these visions of the night, were of a practical turn of mind. Suetonius, the historian, a friend of the younger Pliny, was interested in a lawsuit. He had a dream which so alarmed him, that he wrote to Pliny requesting the adjournment of the hearing. This reminds Pliny of a dream in which his mother-in-law seemed to go down on her knees, and to beg him not to appear in a certain case. A criminal against whom Pliny was appearing, died of disease. It was said that the phantom of the advocate seemed to haunt the mind of the wrongdoer, threatening him with a sword. "I dare not," says the famous letter writer, "affirm positively that this story is true, but it deserves to be for its excellent moral." We are not informed at what time of the night these experiences took place. This was regarded as of importance. A distinction was drawn between the dreams that come before and after midnight. The latter were thought to be more clear and true.[1]

1 Hor. *Sat.* i. 10, 33. Plin. *Ep.* i. 18; iii. 5.

As to the apparitions seen in waking hours, the same principle held good in Roman times as now. The ghosts shunned living company. Our northern visitants prefer for this reason the evening or the night, when all is quiet. The southern ghost can also come abroad at midday, when the heat of the sun has driven everybody indoors for a siesta. Curtius Rufus, a man of such humble birth that, as Tiberius wittily said, he was his own ancestor, was walking one day at noon along the deserted colonnades of an African city. The form of a woman of more than the customary stature moved before him, and was heard to say, " You, Rufus, shall come into this province as pro-consul." And this came true. Thus the life of dreamland passed into that of reality. Dream or apparition, it was all one. The phantoms that came in the night, seemed also in the daytime to flit through the white porticoes shimmering in the hot light, or through the cooler chambers of the temples, or through the woods with their motionless shadows.[1]

The first and most obvious theory about these appearances was that they were genuine. No difficulties beset this theory so far as it related to the reappearance of the dead. Like many favourite hypotheses, in being lifted beyond the range of verification, it was also removed from the perils of disproof. Hence it remained an article of general

[1] Tac. *Ann.* xi. 21.

C

belief, that the departed can return to the dreams of the living, a belief so nobly expressed in a sonnet of Milton. The following words were dictated by a young widow for the grave of her departed companion. "To the adorable blessed soul of L. Sempronius Firmus. We knew, we loved each other from childhood; married, an impious hand separated us at once. Oh, infernal gods, do be kind and merciful to him, and let him appear to me in the silent hours of the night. And also let me share his fate, that we may be reunited *dulcius et celerius.*" " I have left the two adverbs in their original form," says Prof. Lanciani, "their exquisite feeling defies translation."[1]

No ancient conception is more impressive than that of the furies who pursue the guilty. Whether they haunt the house of Pelops, dogging the steps of Clytemnestra or of Orestes, or whether again they scourge the criminals who occupied the throne of the Caesars, they strike us with a strange and tragic touch. One who reads the *Eumenides* of Aeschylus is at first driven to wonder that Orestes should be punished for his obedience to the injunctions of filial duty. If, however, we place ourselves at the ancient standpoint, our wonder vanishes. The soul of the murdered man or woman comes back and hovers over the couch of the slayer, whether the murder were justifiable or not. As time passed, this

___

[1] *Pagan and Chr. Rome,* 261.

reappearance was thought to be confined to those wrongly put to death. In this way there continued one of the strongest motives against murder that could possibly be found. It was believed that the murderer was racked with dread, overawed by ghastly apparitions, night and day. And the belief brought its own fulfilment. The criminal was in unceasing expectancy, and his overwrought imagination painted about him the figures of his victims. The pages of the Roman historians make it clear that we are not dealing now with any artifice of the Greek dramatists, but with a tradition which had continued in Rome from a past far beyond the first contact with the Greeks.

Listen to the threats of Ovid, directed against a private enemy, threats which were more than a mere manner of speaking. " However death may come to me, I will strive to break from the borders of the river of hell, and in vengeance I will lay my cold hands on your brow. Waking, you shall look upon me ; in the still shadow of night I will seem to come and shatter your slumbers. Whatever you do, I will fly before you in your sight. I will raise my lament. You shall not find rest anywhere. Knotted lashes shall sound in your ears. Torches entwined with snakes shall always smoke before your guilty countenance. You shall be driven on by the furies in life and in death. For life is too short for your chastisement." On the night of the assassination of

Galba, Otho (the story went) was heard to start up from sleep with loud groans, and was found lying on the ground before his couch by those who came to his assistance. He tried by every means to appease the manes of Galba, who seemed to be driving him forth. Shortly before Domitian was murdered, he thought that the Stoic thinker Rusticus, whom he had put to death, came upon him in a dream with a drawn sword, while the figure of Athena which was in his chamber, threw away her armour and leaped into a chasm with her chariot drawn by black horses. But the name round which these legends most gathered was that of the matricide Nero. After the murder of Agrippina he could no longer endure to look upon the sea and the coasts by which it had been done. For, remarked the historian, the face of Nature did not change like that of the flatterers who hastened to congratulate the young emperor on his crime. And some believed that the sound of a trumpet came from the neighbouring hills, and that wailing was heard to proceed from the tomb of his mother. He woke to the awful character of his act when it was too late, and although he was encouraged by the congratulations of the army, the senate, and the nation, he could not bear at the time or afterwards the consciousness of his guilt, and confessed often that he was hounded on by the phantom of his mother, the scourges and fiery torches of the furies. He tried to summon forth her manes, and to appease them by the means suggested to him by the astrologers. But it was in vain. Lucan could see him " ghastly pale at the sight of his mother's torch."[1]

In the belief of the Romans, the right to live was not estimated more highly than the right to receive proper burial. We shall see in the next chapter the thoughts upon which this right was based. At any rate, it was so paramount that even the criminal was not refused the burial ceremonies. If, however, it happened so by any chance, the soul of the dead disturbed the peace of the living. When the mad Emperor Gaius was killed, his body was but half-burnt and half-buried. His sisters, whom he had banished, returned from exile on his death, and they exhumed the body of their brother, burnt it, and buried it in the customary fashion. Till this was done, the keepers of the Lamian Park were haunted by his ghost. Every night something dreadful and mysterious occurred in the house in which he was slain, until it was burnt down.[2]

Pliny used to correspond with Licinius Sura in matters of scientific interest. In one of his letters he gives us what is, perhaps, the best Roman ghost story. As so often happens, Pliny could not give this at first hand, but he assures that it rested on excellent authority. There was a large mansion at

[1] Ovid, *Ibis*, 156 ff. Suet. *Otho*, 7. Dio C. lxvii. 16. Tac. *Ann.* xiv. 10.　　　　[2] Suet. *Gaius*, 59.

Athens, which was notorious for its unhealthiness. When all was quiet at night, noises as of iron were heard, and, if you listened carefully, rattling of chains seemed to come gradually near. Then the ghost appeared! An old man, wasted and squalid, with long flowing beard and towzled hair. He had fetters on his ankles, and chains on his wrists, and kept shaking them. The occupants were kept awake all night in a state of terror. Want of sleep produced illness, and, as their alarm grew, death came to release them. For in the daytime, although the ghost was gone, the memory of the figure persisted. The house was deserted, and left entirely to the occupancy of the ghost, *illi monstro relicta.* It was advertised to be sold or to let, if anyone should be willing to take it. The philosopher Athenodorus comes to Athens, reads the placard. The low figure leads him to make inquiries. The information he receives not only fails to scare him, but rather stimulates him to take the house. When night began to fall, he gave orders that his couch should be set in the front part of the house, and calls for writing materials and a light. He dismisses all the attendants to the interior of the building, and began to write, so that his attention should leave no room for empty imaginings. At first all was quiet. The iron rattles ; chains are moved about. He kept his eyes fixed on his tablets without raising his stile, and stiffened his mind to control his hearing. The noise became more frequent; approached; seemed to be on the threshold, and now to have passed it. He looks up. He sees and recognises the phantom described to him. It stood and made a gesture as though it summoned him. The philosopher, with a coolness for which, unfortunately, he himself was the only evidence, motioned to the ghost to wait a moment, and began writing again. The ghost replied by rattling his fetters over the writer's head. He looks up, and finding the same gesture made, takes the lamp at once and follows the phantom, which went with a slow step, as though dragged down by the irons. It moved into the courtyard of the house and suddenly faded away, leaving the philosopher alone, who marked the place of its disappearance by making a small heap of leaves. On the next day he went to the magistrates, and suggests that the spot should be dug up. A skeleton is found in fetters, and is buried in due course at the public expense. After this had been done, and the shade was laid to rest, the house ceased to be haunted. This story shows us how the old conception was still powerful. The ghost of the unburied dead torments the living until it receives its due. Burial is as much a means of ensuring the comfort of the survivors as a mark of respect to the departed.[1]

We have seen how the spirits of the dead returned to execute vengeance on the murderer, or to claim

---

[1] Plin. *Ep.* vii. 27.

proper burial. It is natural that means should be employed by the living to bring about these visits, if, that is, any end can be satisfied by them. It was thought that knowledge of the future could be obtained by invoking the dead, and a whole method was laid down for this purpose—*psychomantia.* The means employed were very terrible, it was thought. Cicero expressed the general mind when he was prosecuting Vatinius. He charged him with practising unheard of and wicked rites, with summoning the souls of those below, and sacrificing boys to the shades. The scandalmongers who charged Piso with the poisoning of Germanicus attempted to excite suspicion against him by similar accusations. Human remains, it was said, such as necromancers use, were found underneath his floors and buried in his walls, so that it looked as if he had been making magic sacrifices to the shades. Yet milder methods than these were in vogue. Cicero's friend Appius does not seem to have suffered from his reputation for being able to call up the spirits. The sacrifice of a cock and the description of magical figures seems to have been enough. Or the strains of a "summoning hymn," such as is still used by modern spiritualists at their meetings, induced the departed to return to earth again. A few months ago, when I was present at a spiritualistic meeting, the clairvoyant girl upon the platform described, to the satisfaction of the audience, a number of spirits whom she saw hovering over our heads. These were recognised from her descriptions as persons who had "passed on." Bishop Bonner came to another seance in Nottingham, and admitted to the company that he was not exactly comfortable in his present abode. There is no need then to seek distant analogies for what is so characteristic of ancient beliefs; they have survived to this very hour within our midst.[1]

Let us turn from the case in which the phantom is of the dead, to that in which it is of a living person. It is to be noticed that the person whose wraith appears is not always aware of this fact. Pliny seems not to have been aware that he was haunting Certus. Virgil in this and in other respects represents to us the beliefs of his contemporaries. The *Aeneid* is not only a mine of the legal and religious usages of Rome. It is filled also with folk-lore. The form of Anchises appeared to his son in Sicily, and commanded him to take a chosen band of retainers, and to continue his wanderings into Italy. Now although the phantom appeared often to Aeneas in his sleep, Anchises himself was ignorant that it was so. Here again folklore refuses the only available objective test, when it says that the phantom of a man can come unknown to him and visit another. Servius mentions two theories; one, that the souls of the dead occupy heaven while their wraiths are with the infernal spirits; while the other

---

[1] Cic. *Div.* i. 132; *in Vatin.* 14. Tac. *Ann.* ii. 69.

is, that a certain power is sent forth by the god which can transform itself into a human figure. This last thought took pictorial shape in the god Morpheus, the messenger of the gods. "No one could pourtray more skilfully the gait, the features, and the voice of a man—to each he adds fit garb and utterances." He imitates men only. Another god, we are told, took the form of wild beasts or birds or of serpents. While a third had for his province earth, stone, water, wood, and lifeless things in general. Although this mythological account is of Greek origin, it answers well enough to the Roman belief. The two theories, that the apparition comes from us without our knowledge, and that it is sent by a god, are combined by Tennyson:

> "As the likeness of a dying man
> Without his knowledge, from him flits to warn
> A far-off friendship that he comes no more;
> So he, the god of dreams, who heard my cry,
> Drew from thyself the likeness of thyself
> Without thy knowledge, and thy shadow past
> Before me. . . .[1]

In the *Aeneid*, Virgil seems to waver among these conflicting ideas. Sometimes the dream is a messenger of deity. Those who sleep on the skins of the slaughtered victims in the temple at Albunea, see in the night the phantoms sent by the gods. But there are two passages in which the poet brings before us traditions of an immemorial antiquity; the

Ovid, *Meta.* xi. 634. Tennyson, *Demeter and Persephone.*

descriptions of the Tree of Dreams, and of the Gates of Sleep.

"In the open court which adjoins the portals of hell, an elm tree stands. It spreads its aged branches with their deep shadows over a huge space. Men say that deceitful dreams take up their abode here, and cling to all the leaves." The dreams, then, are like birds; like that god of sleep who perched on the lofty pine tree of Ida, in the shape of a bronze-coloured hawk. In a fresco in the catacombs of Calixtus, birds are painted symbolizing souls who have been separated from their bodies, and are playing in fields of roses around the Tree of Life. Before the dreams were regarded as messengers of the gods, they were conceived to be the souls of human beings visiting others in their sleep. This elm tree then is really in its origin the home of souls.[1] We shall have occasion in a future chapter to trace the close ties which were thought to bind the life of trees with that of mankind. Hence this elm tree is also a tree of life, like that over which the flaming sword, that turned every way, kept guard in Paradise. The belief in trees of life is almost universal. In Sweden the names of many families are expressly taken from the trees which stand before their dwellings. The family of Linnaeus, with two others, took their name from a lime. It is

[1] The race that first colonized the Campagna was buried in trunks of trees, etc. Lanciani, 254.

said that a branch of this tree ceased to put forth leaves when the daughter of the great botanist died. It is still standing, and held in high respect. Another family derive their name from an elm which used to stand, like the elm of hell, in an open space. There is an old legend of German origin, according to which an ash was the father and an elm the mother of mankind. So also at Rome, a life almost human was attributed to the elm; it was described as wedded to the vines which were often trained upon it. Less than thirty miles away, the Appian Road passed amid the Falernian vineyards, where many an elm supported the rich grape clusters, and may have been thought to contribute to the strange intoxicating power of wine. The lives of which the elm was the home, were lived again in the excitement of the drinker. There may have been some mystic purpose in the planting of elms round sepulchres. When Achilles slew Eetion, he was buried with due ceremony, and mountain nymphs planted elms around the mound which contained his remains. If we may interpret this usage in the light of the ideas we have been considering, the elm tree received the soul of the buried man.

There was an old belief that dreams became false at the fall of the leaf. If Virgil had this in mind, we must understand the dreams to cling under the leaves, not of necessity in the image of birds.

"There are twin gates of Sleep, whereof the one

is said to be of horn. By this an easy dismission is granted to the true spirits. Another gleams with the polish of dazzling ivory. But the manes send thereby false dreams to heaven." This passage, with which Virgil brings to a close the visit of Aeneas and the Sibyl to the shades, is imitated from the nineteenth book of the *Odyssey*. "Twain are the gates of fleeting dreams—these of horn, those of ivory. The dreams that pass through the polished ivory cheat with vain promises, and bring unaccomplished words. But the dreams that pass through the smooth horn, bring sure things to pass when a mortal sees them." We shall see how the images of things float away like films and enter through our eyes, and how influences stream forth on things from the eyes. "By the gate of horn is meant the eyes; which are of the colour and hardness of horn. The ivory gate is the mouth, and receives its name from the teeth. True shades come forth from the gate of horn, because those things are true which we see with our eyes. While false ones come through the gate of ivory, because those things are for the most part false which we hear." An attentive reading of the passage from the *Odyssey* will show that this was the meaning of Homer. Hence when Virgil dismisses the travellers through the gates of ivory, he is reminding us that it is the poet's voice that has given them life.[1]

[1] Taubmann, *ad Truc.* ii. 6, 8.

Up to this point we have not departed very far from the primitive belief, that dreams were caused by the actual visit of the souls of others to our own. The answering idea, that in dreams our own souls leave our bodies, finds little support at Rome in historical times, where living persons seem to have been unconscious that they were entering into the dream experiences of others.

The distinction that begins to be drawn between true and false dreams is a sign that the old conception is breaking up. Before dreams are regarded in the natural and scientific temper of later writers, they pass through an intermediate stage, in which they are thought to be unimportant in themselves, but important as signs of forthcoming events. They are interesting for what they indicate. This standpoint is still that of a large part of the modern public.

The gods often sent dreams, by which they commanded altars and temples to be raised to them. In the time of the Social War, a Roman lady, Caecilia by name, had a dream, in accordance with which the senate restored the temple of Juno the Saviour. One of the most famous stories of Roman history accounted for the repetition of the great games on one occasion as follows: Before the celebration began, and as the people were all seated together round the great circus, a slave was led down the arena, whose head and arms were fixed to a fork-shaped arrangement of wood. Soon after Jupiter appeared by night to a Roman farmer, and told him that the master of the dance had not pleased him. He ordered the farmer to report his dream to the Senate. But even then the government viewed with great disfavour portents and wonders which befel private individuals. The farmer disobeyed the god. A second time he received the same warning, with the threat that evil would befal him if he again disobeyed. Not even then were his scruples overcome. His son died, and the warning came for the third time. He himself became exceedingly weak, and called his friends together. They advised him to go to the senate-house in a sedan chair, and when he had fulfilled the commands of the god by informing the Senate, his feet became strong again, and he returned home. The narrative shows how great punctiliousness the gods demanded in the devotion paid to them. The slave, who was beaten along the arena, took the first place, that which ought to have been filled by the leader of the Salii. And the god, as if he claimed to put the worst admissible construction upon the acts of worship, dealt with this poor slave as though he were the appointed leader of the procession. But we are forgetting the dreamer. His experience was doubtless like that of many another Roman, who saw, in the visions of the night, the admonitions of heaven.[1]

[1] Cic. *Div.* i. 99. Liv. ii. 36.

Let us now see how the Romans interpreted them. When the historian Suetonius consulted Pliny about his dream, he was told in reply that it made a considerable difference, whether you dreamt how things would happen, or on the contrary. From hints such as this we gather that there was a complete system of rules by which the interpretation of dreams could be ascertained. The professors of the art, *coniectores*, were not native to Rome. According to Chrysippus the art was a faculty, which discerned and explained those things which in dreams are signified to mankind from the gods. One, who was about to run at the Olympic sports, dreamt that he was riding in a four-horse chariot. In the morning he visits the interpreter. "You will win," he is told, "for that is signified by the swiftness and power of the horses." He then consulted Antiphon. "You are bound to lose; don't you see that four ran before you?"

Another competitor dreamt that he had become an eagle. "A capital sign! The eagle flies quickest of all birds." Off he went to Antiphon. "Blockhead! don't you see you are beaten? Why that bird is one that chases other birds, and since it drives them before it, it must be last." This valuable information was brought within the reach of the slenderest purses.[1]

There are two ways of meeting superstitions of

---

[1] Cic. *Div.* ii. 130, 144.

his kind. One consists in showing their inherent contradictions. The way in which Cicero deals with the interpretation of dreams in his treatise on Divination is of course unanswerable. He demands a criterion to distinguish between the false and the true. He points out, that although a dream should occasionally turn out to be true, the vastly greater number of cases in which their premonitions are false, forbids us to accept them: just as nowadays the occurrence of even a few exceptions to a generalization of science, throws doubt upon it. But Cicero was in the minority. The dominant school of thinkers, the Stoics, men of the highest reputation for consistent thinking, had undertaken the advocacy of the belief in dreams. Carneades, whom Cicero followed in this matter, was like a solitary and brilliant champion withstanding an army. Being in the minority, he was in the right. But who ever heard of a superstition being overthrown by an argument? This error and darkness of mind must be dispelled, says Lucretius, by the aspect and law of Nature. This he lays down as follows :—" Generally we seem to meet in our sleep the things to which we are drawn by our tastes, or these in which we have been busied, and the mind has been eagerly employed. Lawyers think they plead causes and draw up covenants of sale, generals that they fight and engage in battle, sailors that they wage and carry on war with the winds, we think that we pursue our task and investigate the nature of things constantly, and consign it when discovered to writings in our native tongue." And this applies, not only to mankind, but to all living creatures.

With a graphic touch, which shows that Lucretius had often watched the habits of animals, he says, "Often during soft repose dogs all at once throw about their legs and suddenly utter cries, and repeatedly snuff the air with their nostrils, as though they were on the track of game": a picture that might have been drawn from the terrier lying yonder on the hearth-rug.

The theory of Democritus that "pictures of things and thin shapes are emitted from things off their surface, to which an image serves as a kind of film," puts into a scientific form a superstition of which we find traces at Rome. It was believed that mirrors became worn out through being looked at, as though the images streamed from our eyes. The word for envy, *invidia*, means simply looking upon, that is to say, turning "an evil eye." The Roman farmer knew well the reason if his crops or live stock turned out badly: some ill-disposed neighbour had looked upon them. Lucretius then uses one superstition to confound another when he explains dreams and ghosts by the "idols of things." "These like films peeled off from the surface of things, fly to and fro through the air and do likewise frighten our minds when they present themselves to us awake as well as in sleep." He discloses to us the current beliefs of his day when he proceeds: "I will try to make this clear, in order that we may not believe souls to break loose from Acheron, or that shades fly about among the living."

"Sleep," says the elder Pliny, "is the retreat of the spirit into itself." Like Lucretius, he notices that other beings than man have dreams. He leaves the matter undecided whether dreams bring warnings of what is to happen. "It is generally agreed that the dreams which follow upon eating and drinking, and those which come when we have fallen asleep again, are unmeaning."

His nephew was much more credulous, and we owe to him some of the best stories that have come down from the Romans.[1]

Even Cicero had dreams which events confirmed. When he went into exile, he passed through Atina and spent the night at a country house there. After being awake nearly the whole night, he fell asleep towards daybreak, and slumbered heavily till about seven o'clock. He dreamt that he was wandering through a lonely country in a melancholy mood, and that Marius, whose consular insignia were wreathed with laurel, met him. "Why are you sad?" "I am driven from my country by violence." "Be of good cheer," said Marius, and commanded his nearest attendant to take the orator to Marius' monument.

[1] Lucr. iv. 962 ff. Munro's trans. Plin. *N. H.* x. 211.

"You will find safety there," he said to Cicero. On
hearing the dream, Sallust exclaimed that a speedy
and glorious return awaited the exile. And, in fact,
it was at the Monument of Marius that Cicero's
recall was decreed.[1]

[1] *Div.* i. 58.

THE SOUL

AND ITS COMPANIONS

THE old Romans had a more or less systematic theory of themselves, or *anthropology*. The head was thought to be the abode of the soul, and they took great care lest evil influences should be directed upon it. The life of the priest of Jove was watched over almost as though the common weal depended upon it. He was forbidden to go abroad with uncovered head, and wore a special kind of cap to protect it.[1] During sacrifice the toga was brought over the back of the head as though to guard it against dangers from behind. In fact, the word for head is almost synonymous with life throughout Roman literature. A vow bound the head; the price of the head was the price of one's life. Instead of a 'man accursed to Jove,' his head was spoken of as so devoted.[2] One of the most striking features in the palace of a noble Roman was the collection of the wax masks of his ancestors, preserved in the

[1] Gell. *N. A.* x. 15.
[2] Hor. 2 *Carm.* viii. 5. Cic. *Off.* iii. 107. Liv. x. 38.

atrium. The preparation of these can have been possible only at an advanced stage of culture, and must have replaced an earlier and simpler custom. In later times a wax effigy replaced the corpse on the funeral bier, when decomposition had proceeded too far.[1] I venture to suggest that the head of the deceased man was preserved originally in the wooden cases of which Pliny and Polybius speak, and that at a later time the mask was substituted. I owe to Mr. G. H. Skipwith an interesting parallel, for which he has referred me to an essay on Brittany by the late Dean of St. Paul's. "At the east end (of the Breton church) are the heavy brightly-painted images; in other parts of the church and in the porch, set up on shelves, each in a small black box pierced and sur-mounted by the cross, are the skulls of those who have worshipped there, taken out of their graves when their flesh has perished, and placed on high with their names—*Cy est le Chef de N.*—in the sight of their children when they come to pray. They are churches of the dead as well as of the living." The same words might be used of the Roman dwelling; over against the living tenants there is another company, more numerous, who claim a share in their enjoyments; and as we shall see, come forth to welcome them to the tomb, after bestowing their ghostly presence and help during this life.[2]

---

[1] Baum. *Denkm.* 310.

[2] *Note.*—May we see in this an explanation of the phrase ' os resec-tum '? This is ordinarily rendered ' bone,' and is interpreted as the

In order to understand this and other beliefs, we must clear our minds of many ideas connected with the word "soul." We must not think of it as immaterial. Even the Greek philosophers, for a long time, thought the soul to be air, or water, or fire. Empedocles derived it from a mixture of the four elements. Now if men who had disciplined their minds to connected thinking still retained ideas of this kind, we may be quite sure that the primitive beliefs of mankind would not be less but more gross. It might even be advanced that these material conceptions of the soul are almost universal still. It is unlikely, for example, that Descartes exaggerates the common tendency in this direction when he says: "What the soul itself was I either did not stay to consider, or if I did, I imagined that it was something extremely rare and subtle, like wind, or flame, or ether, spread through my grosser parts."[1] Hence, when stories are told which connect human life in a special way with any material object, we may assume in most cases that the object is thought to contain the life, or that it is actually identified with it. The life is thought by savages to be bound up sometimes, not only with some part of the body, the head for instance, but also with external objects. Stanley

cutting off of a limb for separate burial. With this sense, it would apply as well to the skull as to the finger. On this hypothesis, cutting off a finger is a survival from the older practice of cutting off the head. Cic. *Legg.* ii. 55.

[1] *Meditat.* ii.

gave a goat to an African chief on one occasion. When some missionaries inquired about it afterwards, no answer could be got from the natives ; they thought the missionaries believed the spirit of the chief to be in the goat, and that they wished to get possession of it, and so to control the chief himself.[1] There are traces of a like belief at Rome.

The life of the citizen was in some way dependent on a "genius," while the Roman matrons had each of them a "juno." Mr. Jevons has suggested that the genius of the Roman was really his external soul.[2] It took at times the shape of a serpent, and is so represented upon paintings. Pliny the Elder says that the Romans got the custom of keeping serpents as pets, when the worship of Aesculapius came from Epidaurus,[3] but it seems probable that even before this they were regarded as the embodiments of their genii. They became so numerous, owing to the immunity from hurt which they enjoyed, that, if it had not been for the fires which devastated the city, they would have multiplied beyond endurance.

An appeal to the genius of a man was one of the strongest of supplications ; it summoned his very life to the help of the suppliant. Perhaps the genius of each man guarded him, because its own life was bound up with that which it protected. It was thought to share in his joys, and was even conceived

---

[1] Ward, *Five Years with the Congo Cannibals*, 53.
[2] *Rom. Quest.* pref. 47.   [3] *N. H.* xxix. 72.

to be robbed of its dues by one who abstained from the pleasures of life. "Curmudgeons, *parcipromi,*" says one of Plautus' young men, "wage war with their genii."[1] Hence the Saturnalia, the season of general merriment, was thought to be a kind of holiday for them. When the tasks of the farmer were done for the year, the winter time called forth man's other self, and released him from the fetters of care. Yet the other self was mindful of the shortness of life, not forgetting it even amid the winecups.[2] It was by a change of belief that the genius was considered to pass into the surviving spirit and to become one with it when death came, and the body was dissolved upon the pyre. Thus the genius of the reigning emperor was worshipped during his life, but after death, he himself.

As the genius came to be more and more separated from the man, it was regarded as the companion who guided the star of his birth.[3] When the genius came thus to be looked upon as a guardian spirit, the cakes and wine which it first received as its necessary food were employed as propitiations.

The Roman kept his birthday in honour of this "other self." Only words of good omen were spoken. Frankincense, cakes, and unmixed wine, were offered on an altar garlanded with flowers. The celebrant clad in white, with a wreath round his brows, made solemn prayers for the coming year.[4]

---

[1] *Truc.* I. ii. 80.　　[2] Virg. *Georg.* i. 302.　Hor. *Ep.* II. i. 144.
[3] Hor. *Ep.* II. ii. 187.　[4] Tibullus II. ii. 1ff.　Ovid, *Trist.* III. xiii. 13ff.

The Romans even spoke of the genii of their gods. This custom has not left any traces earlier than 58 B.C., and it may be due to the influence of that later philosophy, according to which the divine nature was removed from contact with material things. The genii, accordingly, came to be looked upon as intermediaries between the gods and man. Preller compares the genius of a god to the genius of a place, as though it were the spirit through whom the god revealed himself to his worshippers at his several temples.[1]

Things and places had their genii as well as mankind and the gods. The birthday of a town was kept much in the same spirit as that of a human being. When Cicero was returning from exile, he was met by his daughter at Brindisi. The day happened to be the birthday both of Tullia and the town. When this came to the ears of the citizens, they celebrated the joint festival with the utmost goodwill.[2] The feast of the genius of the Roman people was observed on the ninth of October, although the city was said to have been founded on the day of the Parilia, Apr. 21. The genius of a place, like that of a man, took the shape of a snake. A wall painting from Herculaneum shows the snake 'twined round an altar, and eating the cakes upon the top ; the inscription runs, "*genius huius loci montis.*" When Aeneas was sacrificing at his father's tomb a

---

[1] *Röm. Myth.* i. 85.   [2] *ad Att.* IV. i. 4.

like experience befel him; he was uncertain, however, whether the creature which glided among his
company was the guardian of the spot or the familiar
of his father.[1]

Buildings were thought to have their genii also;
houses, theatres, market-places, and the like. They
watched too over villages, townships, colonies,
provinces. "Why," asks Prudentius, "do you picture
to me but one genius of Rome, when you are
accustomed to assign its genius to each city gate,
each dwelling, each public bath, each stable, and to
picture many thousands of such beings through
every part of the city, in order that no nook or
cranny may lack its protecting shadow?"[2]

When men were collected together into military
bodies, their union was thought of under the same
shape. Centuries, squadrons of cavalry, standard
bearers, have their genii. The gladiators and the
artisans generally, such as the paviours, or even the
scullions, find a bond of union in their worship of a
guardian spirit.[3]

Thus side by side with the human commonwealth,
there was gathered a kindred one watching over it,
and sharing in its joys and sorrows. There was yet
a third commonwealth; the Good Spirits, *dii manes,*
whose home was underground. That we may the
better understand the beliefs of the Romans with

---

[1] Baumeister, *Denkmäler*, 592. Virg. *Aen.* v. 95.
[2] *Contra Symmachum*, ii. 444.   [3] Wilm. *Indices.*

regard to the dead, let us glance at their burial customs.

They committed the body to the earth originally; burning on a wood pyre being of later introduction. "To me," says Cicero, "that kind of burial seems the most ancient which Cyrus employed, according to Xenophon. In it the body is returned to earth. We are told too that King Numa was buried by the same rite in that tomb which is near the Altar of the Fountain, and it is well known that the clan of the Cornelii have used this mode of sepulture down to our time."[1] Servius says that the ancient custom was to bury the dead in the house. Until the Twelve Tables, the Romans were at any rate buried in the courtyard of the house, and, down to late times, children who died before the fortieth day, were laid in a niche in the wall, covered by a projecting roof or eaves.[2]

According to the more ancient belief the soul was laid to rest with the body in the grave; "*animam sepulcro condimus*," says Aeneas. And the earth was thought to be the actual abode of the manes. "We too," says Horace to Torquatus, "shall join Tullus and Ancus," those kings of old, and Numa by the Altar of the Fountain. *There* is eternal peace, eternal sleep.[3] There was an opening sacred to "the shades of underground," in the Comitium at Rome.

---

[1] *Legg.* ii. 56.   [2] L. & S. s.v. *Suggrundarium.*
[3] *Aen.* iii. 67. Hor. *Carm.* IV. vii. 15. Wilm. 249.

This was kept covered by a stone, *lapis manalis*; three times in the year, August 24th, October 5th, and November 8th, the stone was removed, and the shades, it was believed, came up through the opening to receive the fruits and cakes that were presented to them. These days were attended with complete cessation from work of all kinds. For when the mundus was open, it was like a door set ajar for the gods of gloom and of the nether world. A battle could not be fought, nor a levy held, nor an army start forth, nor a ship set sail, nor a man marry.[1] When a new city was founded, a similar pit was dug, into which each of the settlers cast a clod of his native earth. There were other approaches to the nether world. The most famous was the cave of Avernus, near Naples. It opened wide upon a gloomy lake, and was overshadowed by a dark forest. While the stone of the manes was removed but three days in the year, these portals of Dis were not closed day nor night.

Although life was done with the last breath, the body was regarded as having magical properties, which could be called forth by fitting charms. The Damaras, like the ancient Jews, seem to have no clear anticipation of a life after death, yet they pray over the graves of their parents for oxen and sheep.[2] It was a like belief in the virtues of human ashes

---

[1] Macr. *Sat.* I. xvi. 18. Plut. *Rom.* 11.

[2] Galton, *Travels in S. Africa*, c. 6.

which led the Romans to scatter in the city the bones of a general who had celebrated a triumph.[1] This belief, passing over into the early church, made the bodies of martyrs objects of desire. "Wandering monks sold them; a law of Theodosius forbad them to be dug up and removed for this unholy traffic."[2]

It is interesting to trace the steps by which the Romans passed from the idea of death as a sleep, to that of death as the beginning of another life. Perhaps the typical conception of the Romans was that the shadow lived in and about the tomb, and depended upon the living for some of the enjoyments which gave zest to the bygone years. Hence the tombs of the dead are placed along the highways. As the traveller drew near to the great city, he found the last stage of his journey to be traversed amid a street of tombs, whether he came to Rome by the Flaminian Road, or by the Appian. It was the same outside the Herculanean Gate of Pompeii. All the way the inscriptions appealed to him for his interest and sympathy. "Travellers who crown me and offer me flowers," says Victor Fabianus, "may ye find the gods propitious."[3]. Those who were wealthy left lands and houses, or sums of money, in order that this care for their remains might be ensured. Flavius Syntrophus bequeathed to his freedman gardens, a house, and a vineyard, on condition that the produce should be divided solemnly

[1] Plut. *Rom. Qu.* 79.   [2] Möller, *Hist. Chr. C.* 505.   [3] Wilm. 252.

in his honour upon the Feast of the Dead, upon the Day of Violets, upon the Day of Roses, and upon his birthday. The violets included the stock and the wallflower. "I was talking with a gardener," writes the author of *Verdant Green*, "and saying something about the sweetness of the gillyflower, when the man observed, 'It's a pity it smells like death.' He did not know exactly what was meant, but it was an old saying."[1] Such a belief might have lingered from the use of the flower on the Day of Violets, *dies violationis*. A little child asks its playfellows to gather round its grave, bringing cups of wine, and to pray that the earth might lie light upon her. This, at least, any passer-by might say for the comfort of the dead. Here and there we find a more defiant note, echoing the words of Horace:

> "Blest is the man who dares to say,
> 'Lord of myself, I've lived to-day.'"

A certain Clodius says from his epitaph, in the spirit of Sardanapalus,

> "While I lived, I lived like a gentleman.
> What I ate and drank alone is mine."[2]

But this defiance of death as the destroyer is unusual, and throws into higher relief the yearning for continued existence, however faint and shadowy.

---

[1] Wilm. 313. Mayor on *Juv.* xii. 90. *Gentleman's Magazine*, "Superstitious Customs and Beliefs," 206.

[2] Wilm. 569, 576.

There was a practical reason why the needs of the dead should be satisfied. If they were not fed, they became spectres. This seems to be the meaning of the funeral feast, and the feasts of the dead. The burial rites of the Hindus are celebrated for ten days after death, and have for their object the feeding of the spirit, or, as the later philosophers said, the furnishing of it with a new body for its progress onwards into other existences. It thus becomes a "deva"—compare the phrase *dii manes* —instead of an unclean spirit, as it would be on their omission.[1] When the bones began to appear in the body, as it burnt on the pyre, the Romans said that the deceased had become a god. This may show us why the feast on the ninth day after death was so sacred at Rome, that even the cattle were not put to their wonted tasks, and the legionary was given leave of absence, that he might attend it.[2] The gladiatorial games which were given at the funerals of Roman nobles were, perhaps, a relic of the slaughtering of human beings, in order to provide the dead with their blood. Homer has preserved traces of this savage conception. The shades come to drink the blood of Odysseus' sacrifice, that their life may be renewed for a time, and with it, understanding.[3]

The lying in state, which lasted originally for

---

[1] Plut. *R. Q.* 14.   M. Williams' *Hinduism*, 66.
[2] Preller, *Röm. Myth.* ii. 97.   [3] *Odyss.* xi. 153.

seven days, thus occupied the interval in which the new body was being prepared. Only then might the earthly one be committed to the flames. On the day appointed the funeral train wended its way to the forum, and the body of the deceased was made to stand upon the tribunal, that it might be visible to all. The citizens stood round in a great circle, while the son, or, failing him, the next kinsman, stepped forward and recounted the praises of the dead. But the ancestors of the house also come forth to receive the last "admired guest." The life masks are brought out from the atrium, and men are chosen who are thought to resemble the former heads of the house in stature and bearing. They take part in the funeral procession, wearing the insignia of those whom they represent — censors, consuls, or praetors—and they join the company in the forum, seating themselves upon the ivory chairs of the magistrates in the order of their precedence. When all is done, the mask of the deceased is put along with the others, and looks out upon the family life from the little wooden shrine.[1]

Not merely in symbol then, but in full reality, the ancestors of the Roman lived under the blackened rafters of his home. His thoughts turned from time to time to the reception which awaited him at their hands, when he should become the leading figure in the ghostly procession to the forum. Hence the

[1] Polyb. vi. 53.

anxiety which oppressed him in observing the custom of the elders, *mos maiorum*—those precepts of which the discovery and establishment seemed inspired of God—that he might render to them a faithful account of his stewardship. For they resented the coming of persons who had committed sacrilege, or whose lives had been otherwise stained with crime. When Tiberius died, some of the people prayed to Mother Earth and the manes that he should be refused a place among them, and be sent to join the damned.[1] The books of the pontiffs forbade burial to those who had put an end to their lives by hanging. Thus they were left tossing between death and life, coming abroad at night in their restlessness as spectres. They had no part in the upper air, much as they longed to return to the life they had vainly cast away; and the "good spirits" refused to receive them. "At a place called Four Mile Water, in Wexford," says Mr. Yeats, "there is an old grave-yard full of saints. Once it was on the other side of the river; but they buried a rogue there, and the whole graveyard moved across in the night, leaving the rogue-corpse in solitude." It would have been easier, seemingly, to move merely the rogue-corpse, but perhaps his touch would have been a pollution.[2] The solemn funeral of the noble Roman, and the

---

[1] Cic. *de domo sua*, I. Suet. 75.

[2] Serv. *ad Aen.* xii. 603; *Aen.* vi. 436. *Irish Fairy Tales*, 214. Religion authorised by *mos maiorum*, Cic. *harusp. res.* 18.

gathering of his ancestors to receive him, made his welcome certain amid the ghostly company.

The first attitude of primitive man to his dead seems to have been one of almost unmixed terror. Hence his care to employ every means by which they might be laid to rest. The Damaras sew up their dead in bags, and jump backwards and forwards over the grave, "in order," says Mr. Galton, " to keep the disease from rising out of it,"[1] more probably to prevent the spirit of the dead from rising and bringing the disease. So at Rome the restless spirits of the dead wander about by night, causing men to pine away, or bewitching them into madness. The explanation of death which commended itself to the Roman was that the life or soul had been enticed away by the ghosts. " The Indians of the Amazon," says Wallace, " scarcely seem to think that death can occur naturally, always imputing it to direct poisoning, or to the charms of some enemy, and on this supposition will proceed to avenge it." Death, then, is unnatural, and would never occur, so the Romans seem to have thought, except by accident, or the interference of some evil spirit.

An ancient ritual prescribed for the Feast of Spectres, Lemuria, at the middle of May, is directed manifestly to releasing the souls of the household from the power of the ghosts. " In the depth of night," says Ovid, " when quietness is given for sleep,

---

[1] *Travels in S. Africa,* c. 6.

when we hear no more the baying of the dogs nor the cry of the birds, the man who is faithful to the rites of old, and fears the gods, rises from his couch. He is barefoot. Lest the unsubstantial shadow should steal upon him, he snaps his fingers. Thrice he washes his hands from all stain in spring water. He turns and takes the black beans in his mouth. Then he casts them over his shoulder, and while he does this he says: 'These I offer; with these beans I redeem myself and my house.' So he speaks nine times, and does not look behind him. The shadow is thought to pick up the beans and to follow unseen. Again he touches the water, and rattles the copper from the mine, and he implores the shadow to go forth from his roof. After saying nine times, 'Come forth, spirits of my fathers,' he looks back, and accounts the rite duly performed."[1]

Here we have in a brief compass the main outlines of the Roman belief in spirits, and we see that fear was the prevailing sentiment, even towards those of their ancestors. From all time the hours of darkness have been the heyday of the ghosts. "At night," they say, "we wander far and wide, for night frees the shadows from their prison. Our laws bid us return to the Lake of Forgetfulness at daybreak."[2] While they are abroad the soul of the passer-by is

---

[1] Ovid, *Fasti*, v. 429 ff. Nothing might be done when spirits were abroad. L. & S. s.v. iustitium.

[2] Propert. V. vii. 89.

under great risks. The midnight celebrant snaps his fingers in order to protect his soul from their enticements. According to Mr. Pratapa-candra Ghosha, immunity from evil spirits is secured by snapping the fingers towards ten different directions.[1] When, therefore, the Roman sought to secure rest for the souls of the dead, it was that he might be preserved from the perils they brought in their wanderings. " Once upon a time," says Ovid, " the great feast of the dead was not observed, and the manes failed to receive the customary gifts, the fruit, the salt, the corn steeped in unmixed wine, the violets. The injured spirits revenged themselves on the living, and the city was encircled with the funeral fires of their victims. The townsfolk heard their grandsires complaining in the quiet hours of the night, and told each other how the unsubstantial troop of monstrous spectres rising from their tombs, shrieked along the city streets, and up and down the fields." [2]

Pliny says that the beans are used in making sacrifices to the dead, *parentando,* because the souls of the dead are in them. In the rite described by Ovid, they are given in the place of the living, while the sorceress, mumbling her incantations, takes beans in her mouth that she may work upon the souls of her victims.[3] These beliefs are connected in part with

[1] *Hinduism,* 132.
[2] *Fasti,* ii. 549–554.
[3] Pliny, *N. H.* xviii. 118–119. Ovid, *Fasti,* ii. 576.

the form of the bean-flower : Varro tells us that characters of mourning, *litterae lugubres*, are found upon them, "like to that sanguine flower inscribed with woe." As the Roman saw a field of beans in bloom, he would imagine the souls of the dead to be passing into them. Hence the dreams which followed upon eating beans, a dream consisting sometimes in the visit of other souls to our own. Since the beans contain the souls of the dead, "it seems probable," as Mr. Jevons remarks, "that the object of eating beans at funeral banquets was to convey the powers of the deceased to his kinsmen." This explains further why beans were thought to be a strengthening food.[1] The Flamen Dialis "never stepped upon a tomb nor touched a corpse." Whatever risks he ran then were repeated in the neighbourhood of the bean ; hence he was forbidden to eat of it, or even to name it.[2]

It is important, evidently, that the spirits of the deceased ancestors should not be seen ; they are always eager to gain over new recruits for their mystic community. This danger seems to have begun from the moment of death. The Roman who put the torch to the funeral pyre of his kinsman did so with averted eyes.[3] Thus, whether he performed the last offices for the deceased, or went out at midnight to charm the souls of his ancestors forth from

---

[1] *Rom. Qu.* pref. 92. Macr. *Sat.* I. xii. 33.
[2] Gell. *N. A.* x. 15.
[3] Virg. *Aen.* vi. 224.

the dwelling, he avoided looking upon them. The ghosts, in their turn, did not appear when they were likely to be seen by many; they came abroad usually at night, but sometimes the loneliness of the streets tempted them, when every one was indoors taking a siesta. Under the throbbing glare of the midday sun the "pale phantoms" flitted across the market places and the open roads. In fact, they shrank from being seen about almost as much as the living from seeing them. "Upon the eve of the festival of St. Ives in Tréguier," says M. Renan, "the people assembled in the church, and on the stroke of midnight the saint stretched out his arms to bless the kneeling congregation. But if among them all there was one doubting soul, who raised his eyes to see if the miracle really did take place, the saint, taking just offence at such a suspicion, did not move." The danger of seeing a spirit came to be explained as due to his displeasure, not to the actual effect of the vision.

When the custom prevailed of burning the body, the thought upon which the beliefs just described depend, namely, that the man's self did not perish altogether, was set in sharp relief. The handful of ashes surely could not stand for the whole being of the friend committed to the flames. "The good spirits live, indeed," cries Propertius; "death is not the end; the wan shade escapes from the dying embers." "The earth holds my body," says a slave, "the stone my name; my breath has gone into the air." So too the life of Dido "passed away into the winds." After the funeral of Augustus, a man of praetorian rank swore that he had seen the form of the prince on its way to heaven.[1] The same thought, developed under the influence of the later Greek philosophy, takes a noble expression in the poetry of Lucan. The death of Pompey is being recounted:

"His spirit could not rest in the glowing embers, nor scanty ashes contain that mighty shade. He sprang forth from the fires, and leaving the body beneath, which they had but half devoured, and the lowly pyre, he rose to the sphere of heaven. Where the dark air is joined to the poles that bear the stars —the space that lies between the earth and the journeyings of the moon—*there* dwell those spirits almost divine, whose burning virtue kept them pure in life, prepared them for the lowest shores of aether, and brought them to the everlasting spheres. Not by fragrant spices on the pyre, nor by much gold, can man come thither! When he had filled his soul with the true light, gazing with awe upon the planets and the stars of the firmament, he looked upon the night in which our days are spent, and laughed at the insult done to his body."[2]

Philosophy, however, was well-nigh confined to a few. Often it is the blending of Greek folklore with

---

[1] Prop. V. vii. 1. Wilm. 598. *Aen.* iv. 705. Suet. *Aug.* 100.
[2] *Pharsal.* ix. 1–14.

Roman that is found to have passed from the poets to common life. "The shadow has left the body, and makes its way to Dis below," says one. "Now I am given to the house of Dis," laments another, "and there I shall remain for long ages, brought thither by the flames of death and by the Stygian river."[1]   Only one or two could rise, like Pompey, triumphant over death ; for the most part the Romans held with Maecenas, and preferred earthly life, even at its worst, to the shadows of the under world.   The melancholy that breathes through these epitaphs is summed up in the words of the great minister of Augustus.[2]

"Though I lose strength from hand and foot and hip ;
  Though my form be bent, and the teeth be shaken from my
      gums,
  While life remains 't is well.
Let me live on, though I were fixed to the sharp cross."

USQUE ADEONE MORI MISERUM EST?

[1] Wilm. 580 ; 560.
[2] Qu. Seneca, *Ep.* 101.

THE WORLD AROUND

IF we wished to understand the great superiority of the Greek imagination over the Roman, we could not do better, perhaps, than turn to the idea the early Roman had of the world in which he lived. For evidence we are confined to his language. The figures of his mythology seem to have been only abstractions fixed for ever in some one act or function, and were never built up into an orderly procession, such as that which Hesiod unrolls before us in his *Theogony*. He seems to have regarded the earth as a circle, *orbis*, of which the sun makes the circuit, *annus*. The journey of the sun is toilsome and he flags sometimes. In this he is imitated by the luminary, *luna*, of the night. The Romans observed the evening and the morning star, and thought that there were seven ploughing oxen who continued round the pole that agriculture which was his business on the plains of Latium. Thus shadowy was the reflection which his soul caught from the majestic pomp of nature. For him the world was unrealized. *In vain through every changeful year did Nature lead him.* He could be aroused from his unregarding mood by terror alone. It would almost seem as if the purity of vision which is needed that we may contemplate natural beauty, can be attained only when the mind has been purged of some of its dross. The miracles and portents of which Roman history is full were preparing the way, by the alarm they occasioned, for a more wholesome outlook upon the world.

In trying to imagine how the Roman thought and felt we must allow due importance to the constant apprehension of danger. He was beset on all sides by imaginary foes. The restless spirits of the dead, the evil eye of the living, threatened him and his. And the actual harm that overtook him was but an instalment of that against which he had to guard. Lucretius personifies this dread as religion towering to the clouds and trampling upon mankind. But the alarms of which he speaks found their expression rather than their cause in religious beliefs. A later poet is more just to religion. There is one kind of happiness, Virgil tell us, which comes when increasing knowledge has dispelled every terror, and the dread of the future, and the deafening roar of the River of Death. Yet there is a happiness sweeter still when Nature retains some of its mystery, and we come to know "the gods of the country side." Although the records of the pontiffs, with their tales of miracles and prodigies, stood in close relation to the main current of religious belief at

Rome, there was something in these occurrences which appeared abnormal to the Roman. It was his settled wish to obtain and to live in " the peace of the gods "; *pax deum*, to use the beautiful phrase of ritual. The events of which Livy records so many were therefore to be regarded as somewhat exceptional, and it would be a mistake to suppose that the fashion in which the old Roman viewed the world was always as distorted as might appear from such narratives. We must be careful not to ascribe to him a scientific temper, however. It might be maintained that the course of Nature presented itself then as a succession of events without internal connection, just as, nowadays, some people see in every occurrence an interference of Providence.[1]

The clear Italian sky was not always without a stain to break upon its deep blue colour; nor did the sun shine always with unchanged clearness. Sometimes it turned to blood, or two and even three suns were seen together. Once at Frosinone a halo appeared round the sun, and then the orb grew until it embraced the halo. When the young Octavius entered Rome after the assassination of Caesar, a like circle of light was observed. At Atri an altar was seen in the heaven and phantoms of men stood round it in white robes: *forms uncouth of mightiest power for admiration and mysterious*

[1] Most of the events referred to here are recorded in Livy. See the indices of Weissenborn (Teubner).

rwe. A great fleet of ships, again, was seen overhead at Cività Lavigna, and in Rome a mirage of vessels appeared to blaze in the sky. Many declared, on another occasion, that they saw legions of soldiers upon the hills across the Tiber. The citizens rushed to arms. But those who were on the spot said that no one had been there except the men who cultivated the soil. A short time before the civil wars the gods were observed to be in conflict upon the plains of Campania. At first loud noises were heard, and soon the news came from all sides that two lines of combatants had been fighting for some days. After the battle the tracks of foot soldiers and of cavalry were visible over all the ground. "On the day of the battle of Bothwell Brig, Mr. Cameron, minister of Lochend in Kintyre, had a clairvoyant view of the fight. I see them (the Whigs) flying as clearly as I see the wall,' he said; and as nearly as could be calculated the Covenanters ran at that very moment." Nor have modern and enlightened times been without wonders of the other kind. On August 1st, 1657, Ambrose Rhodes, professor of natural philosophy at Christiania, observed a fine aurora borealis, and prophesied therefrom the political changes which took place in Denmark three years later. We have this from Pontoppidan, Bishop of Bergen, who is the chief authority upon the sea serpent.

The destruction caused by lightning seems to have

been regarded always as possessed of special meaning, and accounts for a large proportion of the
prodigies recorded by Livy. Many of the details
in the worship of Jupiter have reference to his
character as the god of lightning. It may have
been a certain resemblance to lightning that caused
other appearances to attract attention. At Sezza,
in the Pomptine marshes, a torch was waved from
one end of the heavens to the other. At Anagni,
flames were scattered over the heavens, and then
drawn together into one mighty torch. At Falerii,
the heavens opened, and a mighty light blazed forth
from their depths. In contrast to these bright appearances, night sometimes settled over the land at
midday.

Sometimes the sense of hearing was the vehicle
of these portents. Strange voices were heard proceeding from woods and groves in the silence of
the night. Amid the mountains, utterances seemed
to come from heaven, and they could at times be
interpreted into a demand for certain acts of worship.
Before the Gauls came, a poor Roman, as he walked
down the New Road, heard a voice louder than that
of man, bidding him warn the magistrates that the
Gauls were at hand, and that the walls and gates
ought to be repaired. When the Latins were setting
fire to Casale di Conca, and approached the temple
of the goddess Matuta, an appalling cry came from
the sacred precincts, and, with threats, commanded

1em to remove their torches. While it was a
equent occurrence for dreadful sounds to be
eported from Juno's temple at Città Lavigna.

Roman curiosity was excited, and sometimes alarm
as aroused, by the behaviour of animals in their
ifferent kinds. No one need mistake the interest
f Virgil in the life of insects. We find many
tories relating to their prophetic instincts. Cicero
ells us that if a swarm of bees should settle upon
1e stage or the seats at the games, the haruspices
ould have to be summoned. The actions of animals
sed in the solemn sacrifices were carefully watched.
ny sign of willingness or shrinking was an omen
or good or bad. It is solemnly recorded that an ox
nce went upstairs in a house in the Roman cattle
1arket—" of its own accord," says the chronicler—
nd, alarmed by the noise of the occupants, threw
self down, presumably by the window. In another
uarter of Rome, the Keels, two tame cattle went
pstairs and out upon the tiles. When the precious
1etals of the temple treasuries were carried off by
avens or by mice, it was thought that these creatures
ere changing their diet !

The mysterious life of trees seemed, as we have
lready seen, to be bound up in some way with that
f mankind; we shall see in the sequel how this
elief gave rise to numerous rites and feasts. How
onderful it must have seemed when green wood
aught fire in Apulia, or when laurels grew up from

the deck of a man-of-war! Even when the wood was cut off from its parent stock, it retained strange virtues; as a horseman went his round along a rampart, the staff in his hand blazed forth.

It is comprehensible that the objects which were stored in the shrines of the gods, should catch something of their presence. The spear of Mars was distinguished for its liveliness. But more cumbrous objects still had power of motion, and these not always of a sacred character. At Rieti, a rock was seen to flutter, *volitare*. But this is matched by an occurrence reported from Spraiton in 1682. "A barrel of salt, of considerable quantity, hath been observed to march from room to room without any human assistance."[1]

The importance of blood in ancient ritual is so great, that we are not surprised to find that the excited imagination detected its presence under strange conditions. In times of terror it seemed to be over everything. The rivers flowed with it, and the fountains. Sometimes it would rain blood for two days together. Lakes turned into blood. It flowed even from the family hearth; this unpleasant experience befell a Roman citizen for two days and nights. In the grove of Feronia for a day and a night, four statues sweated blood. Even the corn turns to blood. When it is not raining blood, it rains stones, or chalk, or milk, or even flesh.

---

[1] Lang, *Cock Lane*, 122.

To tell the truth, the superstitious fancy is often diseased. We cannot breathe in its atmosphere, and turn with a long breath of relief to the fresh air of wholesome and regular life. Roman imagination, when it was excited, looked out upon the visions of the madhouse; we do not catch many glimpses of *magic casements opening on the foam of perilous seas.*

Occurrences like these presented little difficulty to the general mind at Rome. They were tokens sent by the gods or other spirits, which should warn of impending dangers, or of the displeasure of these unseen powers. In this way they were brought into relation with that spirit world, amid which the Roman lived and died. We must not separate these two groups of beliefs. When every event which passed human comprehension, was referred to the action of some particular spirit, the beliefs in such existences attained a strength which now we can scarcely realise. It is only too easy to assume that, because with our knowledge, we could not believe in the ancient mythology, it must have seemed equally incredible to those who had scarcely attained any scientific conceptions. On the other hand we may wonder with more reason that ancient thinkers were able to free themselves from beliefs which seem to have entered into the very fibres of their mental constitution.

We are not concerned merely with the state of

mind to which these things seemed possible. There is another question, did they occur at all? It is easy to dismiss them as incredible. Yet, as Tubero remarks in the *Republic* of Cicero, the witnesses are too numerous and weighty to be disbelieved, and we are compelled to seek the meaning of these occurrences. We can put down something to the natural tendency of a story to grow. Then, again, we may suppose that some accounts were inventions from the beginning. Still we ought not to rest satisfied with these prejudices against the testimony of the pontifical records.

Another objection that may be brought with damaging effect against reports from uneducated or undisciplined witnesses, is this; How far are we justified in assuming that they were enabled to report with accuracy what they saw and heard? When it is remembered that observations, in the scientific sense of the word, have only begun to be taken since a quite recent date, we shall estimate more correctly the assertions of persons to whom the very idea of accuracy must have been altogether strange.

It is instructive to apply these tests to the records of Livy. We might have expected beforehand that the wonders—miracles in the strict sense of the word—which he recounts, would have been of a more or less fantastic and seemingly impossible character. Nothing of the kind. They are nearly all of them credible and possible. Even the stories about the appearance of the blood admit of explanation.

The chief characteristic of these stories in the eyes of a modern is that they should have been regarded as wonderful at all, as indicating some special movement among the spirits. How are we to explain this? In the first place, the Roman Government seems always to have exercised a very strict censorship upon the growth of miraculous reports. The witness of a strange event shrank from reporting it. For he ran the risk of being imprisoned as a meddler in state matters.

In the second place, the legal genius of the Roman nation provided in its courts of justice a school of evidence, which was only second, in the discipline it afforded, to modern scientific procedure. To hear what might be said on this side and that, and then to test the whole by reference to positive records and positive experience, supplied standards of probability which were of use elsewhere. The Court of the Pontiffs seems to have admitted to the sacred records only such statements as stood very rigorous examination. For the list of prodigies is less striking by what it inserts, than by what it omits. These officers of the state religion must have declined to receive a huge mass of fables, such as those which form so large a part of the mediæval lives of the saints, fables which, we know from other sources, must have arisen on the soil of Italy, in the earlier ages of its history.

Even the comparatively sober narratives which we are considering, were limited to periods of popular excitement. Livy notes this fact as having some bearing upon them. It seems from certain passages in his history that the Roman administration could only then be compelled to take any notice of them, and that its main concern was not so much with the meaning of these miracles, as with the pacification of the public mind. It is usual in some quarters to abuse the Roman Government for its attitude towards the popular religion, as though it were setting the tune of popular feeling. We must always bear in mind that religious belief at Rome was far stronger than appears from the literature taken by itself. If we had all the facts before us, we should doubtless see better why the Senate viewed this important element in the national life with apprehension, and as something to be kept under careful control.

Here, then, we find marked that distinction which has already been drawn between the ideals of the governing body, and the great mass of the people. Livy, coming to Rome with something lingering in his heart of the old beliefs and ideas of provincial life, was perplexed by the contrast. He looked backwards to find an age in which this contrast did not exist. "I am not ignorant," he says, "that wonders have ceased to be announced publicly, and to be entered in our public records; owing to that carelessness which leads men to believe that the gods conceal the future from them. I leave it to others," he exclaims, "to mock those who reverence the past,"—(the past, that is, seen through the atmosphere of the religious fancy). "For if, as learned men feign rather than know, there should be somewhere a City of the Wise"—wise men, who perhaps have thrown aside their fathers' beliefs, "the princes of such a city would not be more sober or less ambitious, the people of such a city would not lead better lives than in old Rome." And yet the spirit that questions finds a voice in the historian, too. "Superstition," he remarks, "sees the interference of the gods in trifling matters. When the mind is swayed by religious excitement, marvellous reports find currency, and are believed without due consideration. Nay, the very faith of simple-hearted and religious men increases the number of these stories." And so Livy is compelled, almost against his will, to justify the traditional attitude of the government.

We may suspect that the leading men at Rome had made up their mind upon these things more than a century before Livy's time, ever since the incoming and partial triumph of Greek ways of thinking. We should not go very far wrong if we let Cicero speak for them :—

"The Senate hears, it may be, that there has been

a shower of blood, or that the statues of the gods have sweated. You do not think, do you, that Thales or Anaxagoras, or any man of science at all would have believed such reports? Blood and sweat can only come from a body of some kind. It may have been some discoloration caused by earthy matter that looked like blood; and moisture such as we see on plastered walls in the street when the sirocco blows, suggested sweat. Besides, these things seem of more importance when people are alarmed in time of war, while in time of peace they pass unnoticed. They are believed more readily, and invented with more safety, in times of fear and danger. Mice, we are told, nibbled the shields at Lanuvium before the Marsic war. As if it mattered whether the mice, that are always gnawing something night and day, nibbled shields or sieves. They have been at my copy of Plato's *Republic* lately. Am I, therefore, to alarm myself about politics?"

If, however, we wished for someone to represent the general opinion, it would be safer to take Livy than Cicero. At the end of the republic, it seemed, indeed, that the spread of Greek thought among the Romans, was freeing them from the burden of these superstitious fears. But this is an illusion created by literature. The great writers of Rome, like those of Athens, were in imperfect sympathy with their contemporaries. They were admired without being understood altogether; and where they were understood, they did not always command assent. The individual could not be explained altogether from the conditions of his time, and—what is perhaps more important here—the time could not be interpreted through any single writer, or, indeed, group of writers; least of all through those of the greatest eminence. They conduct us too far from the general level of thought and action.

On the other hand when the most brilliant period of literary production had passed away, and what is sometimes called *decadence* had set in, we find ourselves under the guidance of men who move along more familiar courses. They are closer to that common temperament and order of mind which may be marked off as the social soul. Hence we find that they represent more truly the general feeling with regard to religious beliefs and practices. This change in the importance and originality of the leading writers of Rome, would seem to have taken place without any answering change in the general temperament. And for proof of this we may appeal to the continuous record of wonders which extends right past Cicero into the times of the middle empire. When Apuleius declared in the second century that he accounted nothing to be impossible, we hear in him the voice of the same belief as that which inspired the earliest records.

When the distinction is thus drawn between

Cicero and Apuleius, it is not meant that the popular conception of religion, of which Apuleius is the spokesman, is any truer than that of Cicero. This would be a glaring perversion of the truth. It would be as mistaken as to affirm that the spiritual ideas of Aeschylus and Sophocles are less exalted than those of Pausanias or Plutarch.

Horace, who might seem to have an opinion like that of Cicero, turns out in the end to be a witness on the other side. On one occasion he travelled from Rome to Brindisi with the most delightful company his time could furnish: Maecenas, Virgil, Varius, who after the poet's death edited the *Aeneid*, and other distinguished men. At Egnatia, a town on the coast north-west of Brindisi, the priests tried to persuade the distinguished visitors that the incense burnt on their altars with a sacred light, *lumine sacro*, although no flame was applied. "A Jew might believe this," writes Horace, "not I; for I have learnt that the gods live careless of mankind, and if Nature does any wonder it is not the gods who in anger send it down from their high palace of heaven." The Italian priests retain their ancient arts still; every year at the end of September the blood of San Gennaro, solid at other times, becomes liquid, to the great delight of the Neapolitan populace. Horace's scepticism, however, was not permanent. In later life he seems to have been converted by what he regarded as a providential escape from a falling tree. And henceforth he thought much in the same way about such matters as the average Italian.

Let us now proceed to gather some proofs that the changes in belief were only on the surface. In the spring of 69 A.D.—the year before the fall of the Holy City—Otho set out for the north of Italy to encounter the generals of Vitellius. Just before he began his march wonders were reported of more or less familiar types. The reins of the sacred car in the Capitol were lost. The statue of Divine Julius turned from east to west. The phantom of a man of more than human stature rushed forth from the temple of Juno. Tacitus in recounting these things observes that in less civilized times such events occurred in time of peace, whereas at a later date they were only heard of in time of alarm. The historian had not made up his mind upon the deepest of all matters: "I cannot come to an opinion," he says, "whether human history is guided by Providence and an unchanging destiny, or is at the mercy of chance." Hence his uncertainty with regard to miraculous narratives. Although he shrank from collecting legends as unworthy of a historian, he also feared to refuse belief to accounts which had received wide currency and belief. Sometimes he seems to be disposed to accept them altogether. Let us take an example which is also interesting in itself. "When Vespasian was in Alexandria," says Tacitus, "many miracles happened which shewed that the favour of heaven and the inclination of the spirits was towards him. A poor blind man, well known for his misfortune, was warned of the god Serapis in a dream, and fell at the emperor's feet beseeching that his spittle might be put upon the sightless eyeballs. Another with a diseased hand prayed at the bidding of the same god that the prince would tread upon it. Vespasian consented after some hesitation, amid the excitement of the multitude. The hand recovered its use, and daylight shone again upon the sight of the blind man." The story was still told in the time of Tacitus, by men who had witnessed the occurrence. Royal personages, and especially the English kings, have been credited with similar powers. In 1683 Charles the Second appointed fit times for the Publick Healings in which his majesty, "in no less measure than his royal predecessors," had had good success. At the beginning of the present century Prince Hohenlohe believed himself, and was believed by others, to have powers of miraculous healing.

Over against the standpoint of the populace, which overlooked the normal and customary to fix its gaze upon the unusual and strange, we must set the calmer and wiser attitude of the thinkers who comprehended the universality of law under the notion of a divine or reasonable Providence. Although modern apologists feel themselves summoned some-times to combat the notion of law as expounded by physical science, the early fathers preferred to dwell precisely on this uniformity of history, and found in it a leading token of the truth of monotheism. "One God," says Augustine, "rules and guides the world, although the causes through which he operates are obscure."

NATURE WORSHIP

ALTHOUGH the Roman had not risen to any general conception of the world, before he came into contact with Greek thought, he had made a beginning towards such a conception. The life of Nature affected him as something with a practical bearing on his interests, if it did not stir him to the vivid fancies of his southern and eastern neighbours. With a little care we can glean from Roman literature enough to enable us to enter somewhat into his state of mind. We come across vague personifications, spirits of the woods and of the fountains, which, so to speak, were intermediaries between him and his surroundings. Let us try to form some notion of the way in which they came into his thoughts.

In doing this we must try to project ourselves out of the present into the past of classical antiquity. One main difference at once suggests itself. We must put on one side the modern feeling for landscape, and all that it implies. Mr. Ruskin has marked off what he calls the pathetic fallacy, by which we project our own emotions on to the realm of natural change. Earth, as Wordsworth says, steals something in this way *from pensive hearts*; but it gains something, too, from our better acquaintance with the laws of Nature. The very notion of landscape is somewhat strange, and is, indeed, almost impossible to translate into Latin. The poets specify the various objects in their kinds, which are embraced in landscape. They suggest but rarely that they grasp them altogether at one view. On the other hand, the idea of a universal life of Nature has only become clear since the science of life has attained something like its present stage of development. Only recently have we come to regard the life of Nature as a realm of law. The exquisite adaptation of living creatures, and of trees and plants to their surroundings, the revelation of unseen worlds of life in the microscope; all these conspire to deepen the emotions with which we look out upon the world, and to alienate us from the ancient temper.

The Roman, however, viewing animals and plants, and the operations of Nature, generally, as vehicles through which powers, dimly apprehended, find their expression, was little inclined to dwell upon the things of Nature for their own sake. He tried to read in them the utterances of good and evil spirits, as though all was unimportant except man and his doings, and the powers that guided him. Those whose spiritual sense was keen, could see through the veil and had their ears quickened. To hear the voice of the fauns, to look upon the gods face to face; such experiences, it was thought, were not infrequent, and compelled every mind, which was not hardened or blasphemous, to confess that the gods were surely present. Since rivers and mountains were meaningless in themselves, it came about that they were thought of under the image of the indwelling spirits, and the material use or damage that came by rain, or thunderstorm, or floods, seemed to be the action of these spirits, rather than of the natural objects themselves. The most vivid figures in the Roman mythology are the fauns, the wood spirits, the fountain spirits; precisely those figures which can be referred most directly to the life of Nature.

In a past, that is not very far removed, a great part of Europe was woodland. Gilbert White, speaking of the forest of Wolmer, says that he saw "cottages on the verge of this wild district, whose timbers consisted of a black, hard wood, looking like oak, which, the owners assured me, they procured from the bogs by probing the soil with spits or some such instruments." If we may judge from the prehistoric pile villages of the plains of Lombardy, the north of Italy seems also to have been covered once with dense forests of elm, chestnut, and especially of oak. The Roman beliefs, amid surroundings not altogether changed from this, gathered especially round the forest and the underwoods. The mysterious life which rises in the spring, and dies away in the autumn, disturbed their minds with the presentiments of unknown beings. The black shadows of the groves of ilex brought the cry to the lips of him on whom they stole, "a spirit is here." The solemn awe which the Italians thus felt amid familiar woodland scenery became unendurable when they stepped upon foreign soil. The Roman troops hesitated in the year 310, B.C., before they entered the Ciminian Forest. And when the consul's brother disguised himself and passed through, he was not so much protected by his knowledge of the language of the country, as by the assurance of the Tuscans that no one would dare to pass the barrier.[1]

The business of the woodman was regarded almost as an offence against the sanctity of the forest. The Roman farmer would sacrifice a pig to the spirit of the wood — be it god or goddess — before he began to thin it. In the solemn ceremonial of the Brethren of the Fields, a sow and a lamb without blemish were offered, when in their sacred grove a tree fell through age, or when some laurels, which had been injured by a storm, were cut down, or when some trees had been struck by lightning. "There are several thickets and clumps of trees in Berar, from which no stick is even cut, nor even the dead wood picked up, though firewood is scarce, and timber valuable."[2]

[1] Ov. *Fast*. iii. 296. Liv. ix. 36.
[2] Cato, *R. R.* 139. Wilm. 2881-5. Lyall, *As. Stud.* 12.

When the Romans reflected upon these beliefs and usages, they began to formulate more or less scientific theories. "Trees have a soul," says the elder Pliny, "since nothing on earth lives without one. They are the temples of spirits, and the simple country side dedicates still a noble tree to some god. For we do not reverence the statues which glisten in their gold and ivory, more than our woodlands and the peace that reigns in them. The various kinds of trees are sacred to their protecting spirits ; the oak to Jupiter, the laurel to Apollo, the olive to Minerva, the myrtle to Venus, the white poplar to Hercules." The modern Arabs think of their sacred trees as places where angels or jinn descend, and may be heard dancing and singing. And the Italian, in like manner, seemed to himself sometimes to overhear, or catch a glimpse of, the beings that haunted his woods.[1]

We can trace two ideas which underlie the custom of hanging votive offerings upon trees. The more primitive idea is that the tree-spirit is fed and clothed by what is brought. Single trees all over Palestine are covered with bits of rags from the garments of passing villagers. "The sacred date-palm at Nejran used to be adored at an annual feast, when it was all hung with fine clothes and women's ornaments. A similar tree to which the people of Mecca resorted annually, and hung upon it weapons, ostrich eggs, and other gifts, is spoken of in the traditions of the

---

[1] Plin. *N. H.* xii. pref.

prophet as 'the tree to hang things on.' We find the clue to these usages when we are told that "in Hadramaut it is dangerous to touch the sensitive mimosa, because the spirit that resides in the tree will avenge the injury." Roman sailors used to make their vows before an oleaster that if they returned in safety from their voyages, they would hang their clothes upon it as a votive offering.[1]

From this more rudimentary belief, of which we find comparatively few evidences in Roman literature, we arrive at the second idea: namely, that the offerings come into the possession, rather than the use, of the indwelling spirit. The Roman general who had killed the opposing commander upon the battle-field, hung the armour of his enemy upon the sacred oak tree of the Capitol. So, in the *Aeneid*, Pallas promises to hang upon the oak sacred to Tiber, the armour and spoils of Halaesus. The sacred precincts of the temple of Diana at Nemi were enclosed with hedges; these were almost covered with the votive offerings hung upon them by the worshippers of the goddess.[2]

There was thought to be a secret sympathy between the life of trees and of human beings. When Augustus visited the island of Caprea, a holm oak, which was flagging, seemed to recover itself on his coming. The Emperor, in his delight, became the

---

[1] *Rel. Sem.* 169.   *Aen.* xii. 766.
[2] *Aen.* x. 423.   *Fast.* iii. 267.

owner of the island by giving Aenaria in exchange to the Neapolitans. Livia, soon after her marriage to Augustus, happened to be visiting his estate at Veii. An eagle, it was said, flew by one day, and placed in her lap a white hen, holding in its beak a twig of laurel. The sprig of laurel was planted, and there sprang up a laurel shrubbery, from which the members of the Imperial house plucked a branch before they celebrated their triumphs. On their return from the festival, the branch was planted at once. It was observed that the tree which grew from it flagged just before the death of its planter. In the last year of Nero, the whole plantation died off, root and branch, as though it could not survive the Julian house.

There used to be an old oak tree sacred to Mars, in the grounds of the Flavian villa. At the birth of each of the three children of Vespasia it put forth a shoot from the lower part of the trunk, and these, the historian assures us, were the certain tokens of the destiny of each of her children. The first was weak, and withered very soon. So the little girl who was born then, did not live through the year. The second shoot was very strong and flourishing, and promised great good fortune; while the third shoot was like a tree. The father of the children consulted a soothsayer, and told his mother, on this double authority, that she would have an emperor for a grandson. The old lady chuckled—*cachinasse*—and wondered that her own reason should still be un-impaired, while her son was already out of his mind.

The strange fellow feeling of the Italian trees for Vespasian continued throughout his life. When he was aedile, the Emperor Gaius found fault with his administration, and insulted him publicly. But he was assured by many omens that his rise to power was certain in the end, although it might be inter-rupted. A cypress tree on his ancestral estate was torn up by the roots and thrown to the ground. The next day it rose up again, greener and stronger than ever. The same tree fell and died at the death of Domitian, with whom the Flavian dynasty ended. There is a fifteenth-century story to a similar effect. A shoemaker of Basle went to a new house, and each of his three children chose a tree in the garden. When spring came, the trees of the two girls had white blossoms — this pointed to their calling as nuns; while their brother's tree bore one red flower. He became a preaching friar in Prague, and found a martyr's death at the hands of the Hussites.[1]

The spirit that dwelt in the tree thus becomes identified with the life of those who are its neigh-bours, and the spirit's abode is a sacred Tree of Life. As we have seen, the tree seems to have become a kind of home for the dead. The souls of those who were buried under its shadow passed into it, and were even thought to cling to its branches as dreams.

[1] Suet. *Aug.* 92; *Galb.* 1; *Vesp.* 5; *Domit.* 15.

Although this reverence took different forms, and was not often expressed in such clear ideas as those of Virgil, we can measure the intensity of the feeling by what we are told of the sacred trees of Rome. Here, as in other cities, it was not only a single family whose life was bound up with that of a tree ; the whole community was interested. In the Roman forum, for example, there was a sacred fig tree which never began to wither but that it presaged some event of moment for the nation. In the reign of Nero it showed signs of decay, and there was great consternation until it put forth fresh foliage. There was also a cornel tree on the slopes of the Palatine. This was, too, regarded with the greatest reverence. According to an old legend, it sprang from the shaft of a spear hurled by Romulus. When any passer-by thought that it was withering, he raised an alarm. All the neighbours came to the rescue at once with buckets of water. Owing to its roots being interfered with, it died in the reign of Gaius.[1]

In the beliefs we have been just considering, the life of the tree has been thought of as having an uninterrupted sympathy with human life. In other cases the communion with the magical existence must be renewed from time to time, as though its virtue tended to pass away. The most natural time for renewing the communion is in the spring, when fresh vegetation appears. On the first of March

[1] Tac. *Ann.* xiii. 58. Plut. *Rom.* 20.

laurel boughs were hung at the doors of the flamens, and of the pontiffs, at the entrance of the court-house of the Salii, and in the temple of Vesta. Like our boughs of royal oak they remained hanging until the next year. At the feast of Pales, too, the sheepfolds were hung with branches.[1]

What belief underlies these customs? It must be something more than a mere feeling of protection. The branches seem here to be used rather as charms against evil influences. Let us trace the proof of this. All goods which were about to change owners used to be sprinkled with an aspergill of laurel. We can interpret this in the light of an instance which Mr. Frazer gives. "The people of Nias carefully scrub and scour the weapons which they buy, in order to efface all connection between the things and the persons from whom they bought them." In the Roman triumphs the spears and javelins of the legionaries, and the fasces of the commander were wreathed with laurel. Masurius is right, most likely, when he explains this usage as a purification from the blood of the enemy. The spirits of the slaughtered foe would haunt their slayers, and seek to carry off their life.[2]

By a necessary developement of primitive thought —a topic to which we shall return—these beliefs came to be referred to the existence of spirits, or

---

[1] Ov. *Fast.* iii. 137. Tac. *Ann.* xii. 24.
[2] *Golden Bough*, i. 154. Plin. *N. H.* xv. 135.

rather, beings very much like man himself, with bodies and human thoughts and desires. The awe which the Roman felt in the forest, led him to regard it as haunted by such beings. The wonderful life of the trees was thought to be due to wood spirits, *silvani*, whose life was bound up with that of the trees they inhabited. As time passed, all these wood spirits seemed to melt into one great divinity : "the mighty god and most holy shepherd, Silvanus." Vows are made to him for the safety of the reigning prince. He has a recognised priesthood organised into colleges. The governor of an Alpine province, Pomponius Victor, makes a vow to Silvanus "half prisoned in the mountain ash," that if he is granted a safe return to Rome, a thousand tall trees shall be dedicated to the god.[1]

But we must not let this later development blind us to the fact that we are dealing here simply with a wood fairy ; one whose voice, perhaps, broke on the ear of the traveller as he passed through the forest at night. Like the fairies of northern lands, he is sometimes spiteful. Augustine has told us how, at the birth of a Roman child, three spirits were called in to protect the mother against Silvanus. That he might receive due notice of this, three men would go at night round to the thresholds of the doors of the house. First they struck them with an axe, then with a pestle, and lastly they swept them with a

---

[1] Wilm. 96, 145, 146, 1262, 1734.

brush. The wood spirit was kept from coming in by these tokens of husbandry. For without iron, trees could not be pruned or cut down ; nor the spelt or wheat made ready without being mashed with a pestle; nor corn be heaped together without brushes. The protecting spirits received their names from these three implements : *Intercidona* from the cutting of the axe, *Pilumnus* from the pestle, *Deverra* from the brushes, because they sweep.[1]

In this account it seems somewhat superfluous that the names of the three spirits should be introduced to explain the use of the axe, the pestle, and brush. These are charms against evil spirits and witches. The mother and the new-born child were thought to be in especial danger from them, and this danger continued to be very great for the child until it had received its name. The wood spirit might take it away with him to the woodland. Iron is a well-known charm against witches. Hence, perhaps, the axe. And the use of the pestle is explained, when we are told that it, too, was sometimes tipped with iron. The use of the brush would seem to be partly symbolic, partly effectual in itself, as sweeping away evil spirits. A similar clearance is practised still among the Uapés Indians. "When a birth takes place in the house, everything is taken out of it, even the pots and pans and bows and arrows, till the next day. The mother takes the child to the river and

---

[1] *Civ. Dei,* vi. 9.

washes herself and it, and she generally remains in the house, not doing any work for four or five days."[1]

It is quite unlikely that the Roman peasant burdened his memory with the exact names of these spirits. Like the other names in the pontifical lists or *indigitamenta*, they arose, in all probability from the industry of Roman writers on religion, attempting, we may suppose, to introduce into the religion of Rome something of the definiteness of that of Greece. Yet it is the lack of definite character that strikes us in the objects of Roman worship. If we wished to form an idea of this worship, the wood fairies will serve very well. When we compare them with the typical figures of Greek mythology, we can mark off an important distinction. Like our English fairies, they have no individuality. They are members of a class. They are restricted to one part of Nature; the forest and the adjoining country. Very little is known as to their origin. All these negative qualities are connected with the stage of worship that preceded polytheism. On the other hand, the gods of a pantheon have each a special name with a more or less marked personality. Something is known as to their birth and life. They can operate in many different parts of the world. Of such gods the Romans had some, it is true. Jupiter and Mars answer, perhaps, to the account we have just accepted. Some writers would refuse to admit

[1] Plin. *N. H.* xvi. 97. Wallace, *Amazon*, c. xvii.

even this, and point to the fact that there were many Jupiters, and many gods called Mars. It may be replied that within the limits of a single Italian community these gods do not appear in more than one form. And this is, perhaps, as much as can be said for many Greek gods, who, nevertheless, are regarded as having individuality. Having made this reservation, we can maintain that, on the whole, the Roman religion is, in its earlier form, animistic rather than polytheistic: concerned, that is, with the worship of vaguely imaged spirits rather than clearly marked deities.[1]

Since these spirits were numerous in their several spheres, there was little need to present them under the form of an image. While there was such need in the case of a god. He might be but a sojourner, unless his presence was secured through the portrayal of his visible form.

We must come to the conclusion, therefore, that there was something unreal and forced in the representation of Silvanus as a particular spirit. And consequently, we may not look for a genuine and ancient representation of him. The earliest images, of which we hear, were of wood. Later he was figured with great detail as a bearded elderly man holding fruit in his right hand. A dog is often by his side awaiting his glance.

So many of his manifestations took place in the

---

[1] Jevons, Intro. *Rom. Qu.* p. xxv.

time of Augustine, that the saint declared that it would be impudent to refuse to believe in them. The people of the wood are still to be encountered in Italy. Round Mantua they are described as half man, half beast, something like centaurs in fact, who carry off and devour human beings. In Valsugana the salvanel, as he is named, leads people astray in the woods, who come across his track. He carries off little children; brings them up in his cave and treats them kindly. He steals milk from the farmer. One who had been robbed set before him two milk-pails filled with wine. He drank; was overcome with the wine. He was then caught and bound. To buy his freedom he taught his capturer to make cheese. This calls to mind the story of Numa and his giving wine to Faunus. Like the wood spirits of Augustine's time, the modern people of the wood are said to fall in love with mortal maidens. Paracelsus, with the quaint show of science so characteristic of him, gives the reason of this. The wood spirits are a family in the order of the *Saganae*, or elemental spirits. They are without souls. But they can receive them by marriage with human beings.

There was another company which lived in the woods, namely, the fauns. In the neighbourhood of Rome the country people were convinced that the fauns were seen in the fields from time to time. It was believed, too, that they burst in upon the deep silence of the forest with their cries and merriment. They made sounds as "of stringed instruments and sweet plaintive melodies such as the pipe pours forth, when it is touched by the fingers of the players." Not only were they heard at night making music. Some of the Romans were fortunate enough to overhear them, as they prophesied the future in that old-fashioned Saturnian measure which was the language of the Italian fairy land, as it is of ours. In times of danger these utterances were of use even to the Roman state.[1]

At the beginning of his *Georgics*, Virgil invokes the help of gods and goddesses in his undertaking. Among them he calls upon the fauns as "the very present spirits of the country." Their festival, *faunalia*, took place on the fifth of December, when the year's labours were done, and the husbandman could enjoy his well-earned rest. Horace has left us a hymn for this feast.

"*O faun that lovest the flying maidens, tread kindly through my bounds and sunny fields, and leave me without harming the young of the herd. For a tender kid is killed when the year is done; the bowl of wine flows full for thee, the companion of Venus. The old altar smokes with frankincense. When this feast comes back, all the flock plays upon the grass meadow. In the meadow the villagers and the oxen keep holy day. Though the wolf is near, the lambs are fearless. The*

---

[1] Lucr. iv. 583 (Munro's trans.).

woodland sheds its leaves for thee. The labourer rejoices as with triple measure he foots it on the earth that wearies him."

There was another and more celebrated festival of the fauns, the *Lupercalia.* It took place on the fifteenth of February. On this day goats were killed. After the sacrifice two youths were brought from each clan. Their faces were smeared with the blood of the victims. Then they were wiped with a goatskin that had been steeped in milk. They must laugh when the blood is wiped away. Their name, *luperci,* suggests that the fauns represented by the young men, were thought of as wolves. Their laughter, which was an essential part of the ceremony, is probably to be interpreted as a showing of the teeth, and is thus an imitation of the wolf. We shall find in another instance that such gestures were thought to be efficacious against pestilence. The Luperci drank heavily before beginning the celebration. This may be the foundation of some of the stories about Faunus' drunkenness. They were clothed about the middle with the skins of their slaughtered victims. In their hands they took strips of goatskin, with which they struck at the passers-by. The Roman matrons were not loth to receive these blows as they were thought to render those who felt them prolific. The " fauns " started from a grove on the Palatine, which was called the Lupercal, and made a circuit of the hill, that is to say, of the site to which primitive Rome was confined.[1]

The office of the Luperci was filled ordinarily by men of middle station, knights, secretaries, military tribunes. Antony shared in this wild ceremonial when he occupied the high office of consul. Not only so. He actually addressed a public meeting in the scanty attire of the celebrants. It was then that he proposed that the Roman crown should be offered to Julius. He acted by design in all this. He wished to suggest that the prophetic figure of Faunus stood before his audience. When the theory of Euhemerus was brought to Rome, and the Roman deities were discovered to be men who had been raised to heaven, Faunus, like Romulus, was said to have been an ancient king: the son of Picus according to Virgil, and gifted with prophecy. Antony then would seem to be inspired by an ancient divine king of Italy to offer the crown to Caesar.

In Rome the west wind was called Favonius, that is to say the wind of Faunus (Favonus). This began to blow about the eighth of February. Pliny describes it as the breath that makes the world fruitful, *genitalis spiritus mundi*, and connects it with the beginning of spring. When the wind stirs the corn in waves up and down, the country people near Königsberg say that the wind is driving the goats through the corn, or that the goats are pasturing

[1] Plut. *Rom.* 21. Cic. *Phil.* xiii. 31. Ov. *Fast.* ii. 267 ff.

there. In Lithuania the south-west wind is called the goat wind. It was the pleasant succession of spring and Favonius that unloosed the chains of winter. Then it became the duty of the peasant to offer a kid or a lamb to Faunus in the shady wood. The Lupercalia thus celebrated the coming of spring. Rome was not the only place where they were held. We hear of them also at Velitrae.[1]

In northern Europe processions take place during the spring which bear a strong likeness to the Roman festival. In the Altmark the boys of the village go to the farmhouses with music, and strike the women of the house with birch rods: first the goodwife, then her daughters, and lastly the maidservants. In return they get schnaps, eggs, and sausage, from the mistress, while the maids put bunches of box or other green in the hats of the lads. Palm Sunday, or Willow Sunday, as it is called in the Ukraine, is regarded by many Russians as a preparation for Easter. On this day thousands go to church, carrying willow wands to be blessed. Scarcely are they outside the church doors after the service, when the willow wands are swung about, chiefly by the lads, and let fall upon the backs of those standing by, especially the women and the girls. The cry is raised all the time, " The willow strikes, not I. Next week is Easter." Sometimes the words are added, " Sickness to the wood, strength to your bones."

[1] Plin. *N. H.* xvi. 93. Mannhardt, *A. F. W.* ii. 156.

The blows are given especially to those who have not been to church. In Nottingham, as elsewhere in England, everyone is expected on "Royal Oak Day" to wear some oak leaves until twelve o'clock. Boys provide themselves with bunches of nettles, and if anyone fails to "show their oak" on being asked, they are struck with the nettles. This seems to be a relic of a May-day custom in which the woods were visited by most, and the stay-at-homes were struck that they might share in the virtue of the new vegetation. The strips of goatskin, then, with which the Luperci strike the bystanders, seem intended to enable them to share in the sacrifice which was made for the whole community.[1]

The name of the Luperci, as we have seen, suggests that they were thought of once as wolves, and their laughter also points in the same direction. If this is the case, we have in the Lupercalia a blending of two beliefs, one that the wood spirit had the shape of a goat (this harmonizes best with the Greek idea of the satyrs); another that he had the shape of a wolf. We are told that it was thought dangerous in Italy to see a wolf, and that if the man was seen first by the wolf he lost his voice. In the same way it was thought dangerous to see a faun when he lay in the cornfields at midday. The belief is still widespread that wolf-like beings pass over the country side. In some parts of Germany, when the

____
[1] Mannhardt, *A. F. W.* i. 256.

wind stirs the corn, the cry is still raised, " There go the wolves."

The grotto from which the Luperci started is said to have been the place where the wolf suckled the foundlings. Here, then, we have a story of children brought up by the wood spirits, of the same kind as the tales of fairy changelings which are so common in Irish folklore.

Not far from the city of Rome, in the Faliscan country, there were some families which went by the name of *hirpi*, or wolves (*hirpus* being a wolf in the dialect of the Sabines). Mount Soracte, which dominates the country, was the scene of an annual sacrifice to Apollo. A bonfire used to be piled up with logs of wood, and the wolves used to leap through this without receiving any hurt. On account of this they had, by the decree of the Roman Senate, perpetual exemption from military and other services. Varro explained their passing unscathed over the flame, by saying that they applied some drug to their feet beforehand.

A legend was current to the following effect in order to account for the rite. Once the country people were sacrificing to the god. Suddenly, some wolves came and snatched the flesh of the victims away. When the shepherds followed the wolves, they came to a cave near the mountain, which was well known for the poisonous mists that it sent forth. These killed any human being who came too near.

And, inasmuch as the shepherd had followed the wolves too closely, there arose a pestilence. On enquiry at the oracle they were told that the pestilence could be stayed, if they imitated wolves. The name of the mountain, Soracte, and of the "wolves," Sorani, seem alike to be derived from the Sabine word for sun; in the same way as the east wind is called the sunwind in Latin, *solanus*. Hirpi Sorani, then, means the wolves of the sun-god.[1]

On the twenty-first of June at midnight, fires are lit on the tops of the hills in the neighbourhood of Dublin. A writer in the *Gentleman's Magazine* says that he was a witness of this, and proceeds: "I discovered shadows of people near the fire and round it; and every now and then they quite darkened it. They were not only dancing round, but passing through the fire. It was the custom of the country on that day to make their families, their sons and daughters, and their cattle, pass through the fire, without which they could expect no success in their dairies nor in their crops that year." An Irish custom, reported from King's County, presents to us a horse passing through the flames in the same way as the wolves of the sun-god. As the bonfire was nearly burnt out, "a wooden frame of some eight feet long with a horse's head fixed to one end, and a large white sheet thrown over

___

[1] Plin. *N. H.* vii. 19. Preller, *Röm. Myth.* i. 269.

it, concealing the man on whose head it was carried, made its appearance. This was greeted with loud cries of ' The White Horse,' and, having been safely carried by the skill of its bearer several times through the fire, with a bold leap it pursued the people, who ran laughing and screaming in every direction." On being asked what the horse was for, they replied that it represented all cattle. If we may argue back from this usage to the ancient Italian one, the wolves and the Luperci seem to represent the community in their respective rites, and their actions in themselves have a magic virtue in which the community shares. These survivals of the present day, superstitions in the exact sense of the word, may help us to enter into the mind of the ancient worshipper. What we must observe especially, is the practical character of the old and the modern customs. On this side they were as seriously intended as, for instance, the regulations by which the foot and mouth disease is sought to be stamped out, or as the use of quarantine.

We have thus alighted upon a somewhat striking office of the fauns. Not only are they the spirits of the wood. They are also in their human representatives, the sureties for the continued life of man and beast. It is not difficult to trace the thought from which these two beliefs come. As the embodiments of the mysterious life of the wood, they are also its channels; and can impart this life either in their animal form, when sacrificed, or again in symbol.

Not only was the wolf an embodiment of the wood spirit. Wild birds also took upon themselves a mystic importance in the eyes of the Roman. We find them, and especially the woodpecker, associated with the wolf. The woodpecker helped the wolf to rear the twins, Romulus and Remus, by bringing berries and dropping them into the mouths of the infants. Later writers, wishing perhaps, to explain this connection, said that Faunus was the son of Picus. (We may notice that one form of the legend gives Faustulus as the name of the foster father of the boys). Nigidius was not very far wrong when he said that the union of the two in the legend was because they were both natives of the wood. "Where the woodpecker makes its appearance, namely, in mountainous and wooded districts, there wolves come also." While the faun has many sides to his character, it is the chief and almost the only occupation of the woodpecker to give omens. They come together in this capacity in a legend about Numa, to which reference has already been made. The faun and the woodpecker used to resort to a fountain on the Aventine to drink. Numa, on the advice of the fountain spirit, Egeria, poured wine into the spring. When the wood spirits came, they drank and were overcome with wine.

Numa laid hold on them and kept them fast, although they turned themselves into all manner of shapes. In return for their release, they told him many things that were about to happen, and also a charm against thunderbolts, which was in use in the time of Plutarch. This powerful charm was made up of onions, hair, and the heads of sprats.[1]

Usages and beliefs which relate to the life of the crops and the herds, change their character somewhat when they are transferred to the atmosphere of the city. The townsman is not vividly conscious of their practical bearings. He has recourse to the wood spirits for other purposes. They can help him, as they helped Numa, by indicating the future. It is also true, of course, that the prophetic indications afforded by birds are useful to the farmer. The cries of certain species are said to change more or less in accordance with the weather. "The ancient generations of the crows and of the flocks of ravens were said to summon the rain and the water, and sometimes to call the winds and the breezes."

The cuckoo has a reputation for prophetic lore in England, which extends beyond his being the harbinger of spring. In Italy, also, birds were useful in indicating the future, to others than the farmer. The crow brought good luck to the Roman when it appeared on the left, the raven when it appeared on the right. The slave in Plautus rejoices

---

[1] Plut. *R. Q.* 21. *Aen.* vii. 48. Plut. *Numa*, 15.

in the good omen, when he sees the woodpecker and the crow on his left, the raven and the screech owl on his right. But when the woodpecker begins to tap the elm, he interprets it a token of the beating which is in store for him. When the raven was seen on the left, when it tapped the earth once with its claws, it made the heart of the passer-by to jump within his breast. A woman once sought relief from a board of guardians on the plea of "grief," brought on by a croaking raven flying over her cottage. She was so frightened by this as to become incapable of work. In English folklore the owl brings bad tidings, as it does in modern Greece. "Two spectral owls, of immense size, settle on the battlements of Wardour Castle, Wiltshire, when any member of the Arundel family is about to die."[1]

Birds of carrion haunted the burial ground on the slopes of the Esquiline. The vulture, which was known to feed on the bodies of the dead, was a bird of bad omen, according to Silius. By a familiar idea the soul of the dead was thought to pass into the creature that ate the body, and so we may account in part for the prophetic meaning of the vulture.

Upon this basis of more or less natural ideas, the Roman soothsayers built up an elaborate system of birdlore, to which we shall return later.

There is scarcely a more beautiful thing in the world than water welling up from the side of a

---

[1] Plaut. *Asin.* ii. sc. 1. *Aulul.* iv. sc. iii. Lucr. v. 1082.

hill, or under the trees in a wood. There is a delightful little spring on the green slope between Mapperley and Arnold. The passers-by show their susceptibility to its charms by throwing brick ends and other rubbish into it. If they had lived in Cicero's time, they would have felt the desecration involved in this wantonness. If we feel this sanctity of water under a northern sky we can understand how, in Italy, where the sun is so much stronger, the spring, with its living waters, seemed to embody some magical or divine life. The same tendency of mind which derived the life of the trees from tree spirits, referred also the motion of water to spirits of the spring and river. I was walking with a companion, one evening a short time since, near the stream which flows down St. John's Vale. We thought we heard voices, as of some people on the other side of the river. On listening more carefully, the voices were resolved into the murmur of the water, as it flowed along its stony channel. Such experiences might give rise easily to a belief in water spirits.

Compared with these primitive worships, the cults of particular deities—Jupiter, Mars, Diana—seem like modern innovations; and in their varied sanctuaries they are found to be accompanied by these more ancient local figures. Jupiter shared his home on the Capitol with Terminus. It was the same in another sacred place to which the Romans had frequent recourse. Diana of the Grove, *nemorensis*, was worshipped side by side with a fountain spirit.

The lake of Nemi lies about sixteen miles from Rome, to the east. It fills an ancient crater, the sides of which rise above it to the height of about three hundred feet. The wooded cliffs descend immediately into the water, except on the side near Genzano, where they slope more gently and are planted with vines. Seen from Nemi, the little town which is situated at the north of the lake, the water seems to reflect the sky like glass, and was called the Mirror of Diana, *speculum Dianae*. Lord Savile began his excavations at a place known as "the garden of the lake," near the foot of the precipitous hill on which the town and castle stand. The first trench that was opened, showed that this was the site of the temple of Diana. The building lay north and south in a great oblong enclosure. On the north, under the steep cliff, there was a great retaining wall. While, on the south, another great wall, seven hundred feet long and thirty feet high, ran along the edge of the lake. Here the waters of the lake lapped on angular buttresses.[1]

The lake receives its supplies, in great part, from the stream which flows by Nemi. The fountain of Egeria springs from the rocky amphitheatre which overhangs the temple. The grove also was sacred to her. In order to explain the position of the temple

---

[1] Wallis, *Catalogue Castle Mus. Nottingham*, pref.

of Diana, in the grove and by the fountain of Egeria, the nymph was said to have been the priestess of the goddess.

The baths were opposite to the north-west corner of the temple, and were supplied with water from the sacred fountain. An inscription has been found, engraved on part of a marble column, which records the gift of lead pipes, and of four basins, apparently as a votive offering. Of the votive offerings that were found here, some at least must have been in acknowledgment of benefits received from the use of the waters. Pliny gives a list of the ailments for which the springs of his time were useful. They are valuable, he declares, for the sinews of the feet and hips. They aid digestion and, further, the healing of wounds. Some are specially helpful to the head, the ears or the eyes; the Romans suffering much from weak eyes. Among the votive offerings from Nemi are terra cotta representations of the eyes and ears, or of arms and legs. One represents the draped figure of a woman with the viscera laid bare; this was probably a thankoffering for relief from some internal complaint. At the present time miracles of healing are alleged to be of constant occurrence at the spring of St. Winifred, Holywell, and are referred by many to the intercession of the saint. Pliny, indeed, might attribute the cures of which he speaks to the properties of the water. But most of his contemporaries would regard them as due to the spirits of the springs. In the monastery church of Daphni, near Athens, the icon of Mary is covered with small representations of eyes or limbs in silver and less precious materials. Like these, the offerings to Diana recorded the gratitude of her worshippers for good received.

Outside the Porta Capena at Rome there was another grove sacred to Egeria. It lay not far from the gate on the left of the Appian Road, the traffic of which could be heard in the grove. The well still flows near the Villa Fonseca, and the tradition of its healing powers lived on through the middle ages. The spirit of the well was said to have instructed Numa by night as to the worship which should be rendered to the god. According to one legend, Faunus and Picus did not themselves tell Numa the charm against thunderbolts, of which mention has been made. They drew down Jupiter, the god of thunder, from heaven by their magic. When the king of the gods appeared, the earthly king almost lost his senses in terror. But he was inspired by Egeria, and asked that he might be taught the charm against thunderbolts. Jupiter began by declaring that the charm must be made with heads — "Yes, of onions," interrupted Numa. Jupiter went on "with men's"—"Hair," said Numa. "And with living," — said Jupiter. "Sprats," said Numa. Plutarch remarks that this fabulous and absurd story illustrates the disposition of the men of that time towards religion. Certainly we miss in Roman folk-lore the comedy and even vulgarity that distinguish some of our English fairy tales. But this may be due to the channels along which it has come down to us. When fairyland is put under a system, laughter ceases to be heard there. We can just catch echoes of it in Ovid. But Varro, and Cicero, and Livy take all the old tales too seriously, and when they have passed through such hands their brightness is gone.[1]

Numa is said to have dedicated the place in which he met Egeria, and the adjacent fields, to the water spirit and her sisters, the singing maidens, *camenae*.

Once there was a plague in the city. In the midst of the public distress, a bronze shield fell from heaven one day at the feet of Numa. On the advice of the singing sisters, he had eleven other shields made exactly like it, so that any one who wished to steal it might be uncertain which to take. For the safety of the city was bound up with the shield. The twelve shields were then put in the temple of Mars. After this the disease was stayed. Here again we find the water spirits helping to avert pestilence.

It was from their spring that the vestal virgins fetched water every day for the cleansing of the *regia*, the house of the king.[2]

It has been suggested with great likelihood that

---

[1] Plut. *Numa*, 15.

[2] Ov *Fast.* iii. 357 ff. Plut. *Numa*, 13.

Evander answers in Greek to the Latin Faunus, the favouring spirit. We are told that Evander was the son of Carmenta. She was a fountain spirit gifted with prophecy. Her altar was near the Carmental gate, which was named after her. She is said to have given advice to Evander in oracles expressed in verse. Just as the Muses of Greece, who also were fountain spirits, were thought to be the source of the wisdom of Greek poets, so the Roman kings had recourse to the singing maidens who haunted their springs. In the excitement of worship, Carmenta was said to have lost her reason. Indeed, the name *lymphatus*, possessed by a fountain spirit, was applied to those who were bereft of reason. On the other hand some waters, such as those of Sinuessa, took away insanity.[1]

Other waters were thought to be a cure for barrenness. Hence we can understand why Carmenta was thought to watch over the birth of children. Her festival was celebrated by the matrons of Rome on the fifteenth of January.

While Evander was the son of one fountain spirit, he was the husband of another. Her name was Marica, a fountain spirit of Laurentum. These stories about Evander have their root in the popular belief that the woods and springs were haunted by fauns and nymphs, and express the belief with transparency.

---

[1] Liv. i. 7. *Aen.* vii. 47; viii. 339. Plin. *N. H.* xxxi. 8.

The nymphs were thought to be able to harm. In the curious curses which have been found written upon strips of lead, they are called upon sometimes to destroy a hated individual in the course of the year. On the other hand the Roman farmer invoked the water spirit along with *Good Luck*. The superstitious Italians still drink of the Fontana di Trevi when they leave Rome, and throw a coin into the basin. They think that by this their safe return home is made certain.

The feast of fountains, *fontanalia*, was held on October the thirteenth. Garlands were thrown into the springs, and the wells were crowned. In addition to the flowers, offerings of wine were made, and a kid was sacrificed. Numa, it was said, offered wine and a sheep to the *Fountain*, on the celebrated occasion of his interview with Jupiter. When the trees in the sacred grove were struck by lightning, the Brethren of the Field, among their other offerings, slaughtered two wethers in the name of the Fountain. Not so many years ago the wells at Tissington, in Derbyshire, used to be decorated on Holy Thursday, with boughs of trees, tulips, and so forth, and after the prayers for the day were over, the parson and the choir used to pray and to sing Psalms at the well.

"In the prayers of the augurs," says Cicero, "we see Tiberinus, Spino, Almo, Nodinus, and the names of other streams." But the Romans do not seem to have formed any very lively idea of their river gods, not even of the Tiber. Virgil speaks of Tiberinus simply as the spirit of the spot, *deus loci*, who appeared to Aeneas as he slumbered on the bank. He rose amid the poplars—there are great woods still along the Tiber—clothed in a dark blue cloak of fine linen, and a bonnet of reeds. But the god did not leave his river, and no legends seem to have gathered round his name. When we are told of the bull-shaped Aufidus, we must put this idea of the river spirit's form down to Greek influences. It has been suggested that the famous group of the wolf and the twins, which is in the Capitoline Museum, represents the Tiber, but this suggestion is not, as far as I know, supported by external evidence.[1]

An interesting bust of marble, double like the head of Janus, was found in the excavations of Nemi. It seems to portray two water spirits. They have scales on their cheeks, and the leaves of water plants cover their neck and chest. Fins rise from their foreheads and almost look like horns. One face is that of a young beardless man with small fins at the side of his mouth, while the other is that of an elderly man with beard and moustache. The eyebrows are arched. Their expression is of a certain sadness, as though their prophetic power was a burden to them. We may, perhaps, see in them the indwelling spirits of the lakes of Albano and Nemi. The type

<hr>

[1] Cic. *N. D.* iii. 52. *Aen.* viii. 32.

of the younger face is not unlike that of the head of a river god at Vienna, although the Nemi example is characterised by much more grace and delicacy.[1]

Mr. Jevons explains the peculiarities in the worship of Hercules, by identifying him with the Greek Heracles, and supposes that the genius of the Roman took the shape of the foreign deity. But is there any adequate reason for supposing that the worship of Hercules was adventitious? It was associated with traditional customs, to all appearances, of great antiquity. Women were not allowed to partake of the flesh of the victims offered at the Great Altar. Boys went out of doors to swear by him. If we may accept the account of Tacitus, the Great Altar was included within the walls of the city on the Palatine. It is difficult to believe that the influence of the Greeks was great enough at this early date to bring in a new deity. Although the Roman worship may not be derived from Greek sources, it is unlikely that the likeness of Heracles and Hercules is simply casual. It would seem that Heracles or Hercules is one of those figures which were sacred to the common ancestors of the Greeks and Romans.

Who, then, was Hercules? Perhaps this is one of those questions which will always invite to guessing. There are, however, some reasons which lead one to believe that Hercules was either one of the fountain spirits, or closely connected with them. He

---

[1] Baum. *Denkmäler*, p. 570.

was worshipped along with the muses, and although we may trace this cult to foreign influence, there are other evidences from which we might expect him to be found in the company of the singing spirits, muses, or *camenae*, who inhabit the springs. In this way he helps us to understand, what otherwise might seem strange, the fact that his Greek cousin was worshipped along with such unexpected company.

The Romans found many resemblances between him and the Phoenician Baal. There was a fountain of Hercules at Caere. This may have been dedicated by the Phoenician settlers to Baal, as the lord of the waters that come up from the land. It is curious that neither flies nor dogs, according to popular belief, would enter the temple of Hercules in the Roman cattle market. Tithes, too, were paid to him as to Baal.

One of the few popular legends of Rome that have come down to us, is told of Hercules, and, I think, it confirms what we might infer from his likeness to Baal. When the young Roman asked his father concerning the sacrifices at the Great Altar, we might suppose him to have the following tale told him for explanation :—

"Once upon a time there lived on the Aventine a giant named Cacus, and he used to be a terror to all the country round. You could always see blood in front of the cave, and there were men's heads hanging over the doorway. One day Hercules was driving his cattle by, and the giant took four bulls and four cows and led them to the cave. In order that they might not be traced, he dragged them by their tails, and so their tracks seemed to point away from the cave and not towards it. But Hercules found him out by the bellowing of the stolen cattle. He was filled with anger, and hastened to the place from which the sound seemed to come. Cacus was frightened, and put a huge stone in front of the entrance, which Hercules could not move. However the hero pulled down a rock further on, which overhung the stream, and laid all the side of the cave to view. A great fight followed, in which Hercules came off best and killed the giant. In gratitude for their deliverance from the giant, the country people established sacrifices to Hercules at the Great Altar."

There is an old Latin word for patrimony, *herctum*, with which the name of the hero seems to be connected. Hercules would then be the spirit of the enclosure, genius of the farmyard, as Mommsen calls him. Hence his altar is near the cattle market.[1]

Cacus was a fire spirit. Virgil calls him the son of Vulcan. The story then presents to us a conflict of the guardian of the cattle with a fire monster.

[1] Jevons, Intro. *R. Q.* p. li. Tac. *Ann.* xii. 24. Plin. *N. H.* x. 79. Liv. i. 7.

PRIMITIVE THOUGHT

A GREAT gulf is put between each human being and his fellows, so that the life of the individual runs its own particular course. Yet all lives are cast in one common mould. "The affections of the soul," says Aristotle, "are the same in all."[1] This holds from age to age, as well as from race to race in the present. The comparative method, as applied in historical research, is based upon this fact; that our common nature manifests itself in like ways under like circumstances. By comparing the practices and beliefs of different peoples and different ages, we find them to present certain broad resemblances. Where one set of records is imperfect, we can sometimes fill up the gaps by reference to the fuller accounts of another set. In this way strange customs need be no longer considered in their isolation, but are explained by the beliefs which are found elsewhere to underlie similar customs. Acts, which seem at first sight intrinsically absurd or repulsive, gain a show of reasonableness, when we thus succeed in realising the point of view at

[1] *de Interpret.* i. 3.

which they are done. The most primitive elements of the Roman religion, as of contemporary savage religions, the folklore of our countrymen, or the ideas and rites of the cruder forms of spiritualism, rest upon a theory of life and of the world, which to a certain extent is consistent with itself, and explains, more or less, the occurrences to which it is applied. This primitive philosophy, the root (and sometimes the branches as well) of other philosophies, we will attempt to consider. Though we direct our attention mainly to the Romans, this will not prevent us from tracing the outlines, of what seems to be almost a necessary stage in the unfolding of the human mind.

Bacon caught, in the Greek legends, " a soft whisper from the traditions of more ancient nations conveyed through the flutes of the Grecians." Vico believed that the early Romans learnt a profound philosophy from their neighbours to the north and to the south.[1] It is agreeable to think that there was an ancient body of doctrine indigenous to Rome, which will account satisfactorily for the traces of primitive wisdom which Vico found. There was then, however, no synthetic philosopher ready to erect an imposing structure out of the science of his contemporaries. Such a duty has fallen upon these later times, and has been undertaken with great spirit and some success by the students of folklore. Whether our

---

[1] *Adv. Learn.* ii. c. 13. Flint, *Vico.* 85.

modern knowledge is to be regarded as a degeneration from the ancient, will shortly appear.

The first principle of primitive philosophy is that each occurrence has one cause. It employs a logic, the lines of which are not parallel to modern methods. It is not troubled with the plurality of causes. Latium was at one with our English Arcadians in this. " That's a large question," the Rev. Augustus Jessopp began on one occasion, and was proceeding to explain further when surly Bob broke in fiercely, " There you are again with your large questions. I 've heerd that lots o' times when I want to knaw the reason why. You keep talkin' o' causes when there aint ony one cause for one thing." This old art of reasoning is not confined to Arcady. The Arcadian wanders forth, and takes his wisdom with him. He is great in politics. He can refer all the ills of national life to some single circumstance. " Give me some single reform, and all will be well." He was once as triumphant in medicine as he is still in politics. But the advance of science has given such an unfair advantage to the professional physician that the amateur is beginning to decline the contest. The day of the quack is setting. Medicine, once the happy hunting ground of the discursive reason, is being cultivated bit by bit; and its main thoroughfares are beginning to be staked out. Even the wayfaring man can see that the Arcadian is somewhat out of place here. On the old theories we have only to find out one cause, say the incantations of a witch, or the influence of an evil star, in order to account satisfactorily for a disease, while we may leave out of account such trifles as the constitution, history, diet, and surroundings of the patient. Not only is the diagnosis of the case simplified; the finding of the cure is not less so. Just as that which brings the ailment is one, so is that which will take it away. We may be sure that there is some single drug, or some form of words which will do this. Yet a feeling of superiority is out of place, even in presence of primitive thought. We are all Arcadians, more or less. The only danger is that we may be in Arcadia and not know it.

Arcadia has a further advantage over other countries. Not only is it quite sure, to begin with, that there is only one cause for one effect. What is more, there is always some one to hand who can point it out. Suppose, for instance, that you want to cure the liquor habit. Pliny says that the eggs of a screech owl given in wine for three days, will produce a distaste for wine. This sounds rather likely.

In the same way, when we pass from the ailments of the individual to those of the body politic, it is desirable to find out from some one who knows, what precisely will bring back the normal and healthy condition. In the year 364 B.C., Rome suffered under a terrible pestilence. Other means of allaying it were tried in vain. Theatrical performances were given for the first time, but without effect. Happily it was remembered that a previous pestilence abated when the Dictator drove a nail into the right hand wall of the great temple of the Capitol. The expedient was decided upon.[1] We are not told with what measure of success. After the battle of Cannae, the terrified Romans found a remedy for their misfortunes by burying alive, in the cattle market, two Greeks and two Gauls. This savage expedient was enjoined on them by their books of destiny. We may suppose that they had recourse to written records when their living oracles were discredited.

Arcadia is very contemptuous of persons whom it calls materialists. If there is anything about which it is proud, it is its belief in spirits. There is no need to search all the realms of existence for the causes of good or ill fortune. Arcadia looks for the ghost. In fact it is a Psychical Research Society. In this Arcadia sets itself no difficult task. The dead were buried at Rome in the haunts of the living. Their spirits were always present, and explained nearly everything that could not be put down to obvious causes. If anything went wrong, it was because some one had not received the due funeral rites, or because offerings of wine, and cakes, and flowers had not been made at the tombs of the elders.

We have already seen that disease and death were

---

[1] Liv. vii. 3.

attributed to the restless spirits of the departed, rather than to special disease spirits. We may assume that this is the more primitive form of the belief in the action of spirits. It is only at a later time that special agents are assigned to the conduct of each kind of action, or of each corner of the natural world.

This later belief took a very striking form at Rome. Every single action was thought to be under the care of a spirit. By invoking it, the due performance of the action was ensured. The names of such spirits were enrolled upon lists, *indigitamenta*. These set forth the different series of acts which it falls to man to perform in his passage through life, and particularly, as we might have expected in a people of farmers, the operations of husbandry. The spirit of eating, *Educa*, and of drinking, *Potina*, attended the young child in its home. As he left the house the spirits of departing, *Abeona*, and of journeying, *Iterduca*, led him on his way. While the spirits of approaching, *Adeona*, and of home-coming, *Domiduca*, brought him back again. So in farm life, the spirits of cutting, *Intercidona*, of grinding, *Pilumnus*, of sweeping, *Deverra*, of sowing, *Saturnus*, of pruning, *Puta*, of beekeeping, *Mellonia*, were at hand. In commerce, the spirit of gain, *Mercurius*, was accompanied by the spirit of money, *Pecunia;* and the ship of the merchant was brought to the harbour by the harbour spirit, *Portunus*. A few lines from Plautus' comedy, *The Merchant*, will show how deeply rooted was this habit of mind.

"*Charinus.* 'Who calls me?'
"*Eutychus.* 'Hope, Safety, Victory.'
"*Charinus.* 'Why do you want me?'
"*Eutychus.* 'I want to come with you.'
"*Charinus.* 'Seek another companion. My companions will not let me go.'
"*Eutychus.* 'Who are they?'
"*Charinus.* 'Care, Misery, Sorrow, Weeping, Groans.'"

Not only are there spirits which help man in his work. There are others which bring him harm and hindrance. The cautious Roman took care to be on good terms with these also. The priest of Quirinus celebrated a solemn feast in honour of the mildew spirit, *Robigo*. It is curious to find Mr. Ruskin speaking, in terms that would have seemed familiar to a Roman, of "the spirit that throughout the world has authority over rending rottenness and decay." At first, reverence was paid to these spirits according to their power, and not at all according to their ethical importance. When the passage began to be made to this latter standpoint, the older worships presented a stumbling-block. Cicero applauds the erection of temples to Mind, Piety, Virtue, Faith. "We ought," he says, "to consecrate virtues, not vices." Hence he would put away the worship of the Fever spirit and of Evil Fortune.[1]

[1] *Modern Painters*, iii. 118. Cic. *Legg.* ii. 28.

This mode of thought spread from religion into the speculations of physical science. It was not enough to say that any substance was of such or such a kind. The reason must be that it had certain "virtues." These turn out, on inquiry, to be nothing more than abstractions.

How is it that in modern times we are more successful in detecting the relations of cause and effect? We cannot pride ourselves on having made this progress by the unaided effort of the intellect. As Schopenhauer says, " The connection between cause and effect is really as mysterious as that which is imagined between a magic formula and the spirit which must appear when invoked by it." Perhaps we may say that prejudices of all kinds, conscious and unconscious, stir the mind as it looks out upon Nature for the first time, and that it begins to see clearly, only when it has laid these prejudices aside. At first we must be in a receptive mood, almost passive. Only when we have begun to recognise in this way the more obvious things of Nature, can we use our knowledge as a stepping stone to a further advance.

Again, the possibility of accurate observation is largely determined by the accuracy of our instruments of measurement. In the absence of these, the regularity of natural processes was pressed home upon the Romans with far less force. Instead of natural order being, as with us, the standard of permanence and fixity, it was thought that external changes were almost impossible to discern aright, and that truth could scarcely be attained in this quarter. Some thinkers were of opinion that no fact could be so ascertained, that assent to it was unavoidable. "Accuse Nature," they said, "who has hidden truth in the abyss."[1] In fact, the amount of certainty which is attainable in moral science, was greater than the certainty which seemed then to be attainable in physical science. It is comprehensible, therefore, that the causation, which was found to hold good in human action, should be transferred to Nature. It was a necessary stage in the progress of thought that it should attribute all events, physical as well as moral, to personal agencies.

These personal agencies, whether they are the ghosts of the dead, or the spirits of abstract operations, will feel and think much as those in whose fancies they have their being. We shall find in them a reflection of their human creators.

A leading characteristic of primitive consciousness is that it flows in well-worn channels. The thought and feeling of a savage is conservative to a degree of which we can scarcely conceive. He is the bondslave of innumerable precedents, which determine every act and word. The freedom of unfettered Nature is a modern ideal which, by a familiar inversion, has been projected on to the past. The Romans

---

[1] Cic. *Acad.* ii. 32.

had a name by which they sanctified the adherence to what is old ; *mos maiorum*, the custom of the elders, such was the form of words which they used as a charm against innovation. The emotion which attended upon such modes of life, would be very naturally a dread of change. This was the natural cloak for that leading human passion, the passion for indolence, for freedom from intellectual effort. When this feeling runs unchecked, it soon clothes itself in a philosophy, over which in turn it throws the protection of religion. In this way we reach a grand maxim of primitive thought. *What is new, is dangerous.* More than this, the spirits are offended by it. So, at least, the priestly records affirmed ; but that was perhaps merely another way of saying that their authors did not look kindly upon change. The Potitii, who had an ancestral worship at the Great Altar, handed over their duty to the public slaves. "The consequence of this innovation deserves notice," says Livy, "and should be a warning against making changes in religion. The whole family of the Potitii was blotted out within a short time, and the vengeance of heaven was visited upon the censor Appius, upon whose advice they had acted. A few years after, he lost his sight."[1] And, generally, if other explanations failed, it was possible to refer public calamities to some alteration that had taken

---

[1] Livy, ix. 29.

place in the national customs; some deviation from that which was sanctioned by the practice of antiquity. When the monarchy was abolished in fact, provision was made for its continuance in name. There was still a king; but for religious purposes only, *rex sacrorum*. By this means the State continued, it was hoped, to retain all the advantages that flowed from the old institution. This aversion to change was naturally strongest in those classes whose interest was bound up in the existing order of things. Here they came into conflict with the feelings of the newcomers from neighbouring districts, and, indeed, with the large floating population of Rome.

Men for whom the existing order has no emotional impressiveness, who are not in touch with the sentiments which cast a glamour over it, for whom, therefore, the religion of the State is formal in the main; to them what is new appeals with strange promise. Ordinarily the conservative forces were powerful enough to keep these elements in check. And the Roman Government, when it dared, came down with a heavy hand on the religious revolutionary. In times of national affliction and of peril, things were different. Regular agencies for securing the divine favour were discredited. The revolutionaries were reinforced by the more timorous and superstitious of the general body of citizens, and the Government was compelled to yield.

The new was no longer viewed with suspicion. It was rather welcomed. The history of Roman religion is, largely, a history of changes brought about in this manner. In the second Punic war sacred games in honour of Apollo were established, at the bidding of a famous prophet named Marcius. This was in 212, B.C. Seven years afterwards the excited populace sought consolation still further afield, and fetched the Mighty Mother from Asia. We may suspect that the administration yielded reluctantly to these popular movements. In the year 213 foreign objects of worship were brought in, and were venerated with such superstitious enthusiasm that, says Livy, "either the nation or its deities seemed to have been changed on a sudden." Not only was the ancient worship suspended in private; but even in public sacrifices and prayers were offered in unprecedented ways. At first the sober citizens contented themselves with private complaints. When, however, the lesser officials attempted to put the offending practices down, they almost provoked a riot. The matter was brought before the Senate, and they gave orders to the city praetor to sweep the city clear of those superstitions. He commanded all the sacred prophetic books in the city to be brought to him. But he seems to have overlooked the verses of Marcius. For, next year, the Senate was compelled to accept a new worship, as we have already seen.[1]

[1] Liv. xxv. 1.

If, then, one part of the community saw in their gods a disinclination to change, and so safeguarded themselves against disturbance, another part looked to foreign sources for a sympathy which they failed to find in the presence of the traditional deities. In this way both parties projected their own *emotions* on to the face of heaven. Let us now see how they read their characteristic modes of thought into the pervading *activities* of the spiritual agencies surrounding them.

In the primitive mind there is the closest association possible, between the name of a thing and a thing itself. Those who have freed themselves from the bondage of a single tongue can scarcely imagine how strong this tie remains in the minds of those who know no language save their own. To speak of a thing is almost the same as to have it before you. Mr. Spencer describes the name of a thing as "in a strained sense an attribute."[1] The studies of this distinguished writer have lain mainly in other directions than those of literature. I do not think such a notion would have occurred to a student of foreign tongues. However, if I may without impertinence use this illustration, it seems to me to explain very well the attitude of the Roman mind towards names. To the Roman the name was an attribute; and this, not in any strained sense, as Mr. Spencer views it in the course of a special

[1] *Princ. Psych.* pt. vi. c. 9.

argument. It was rather the leading attribute, and for some purposes might be treated as equivalent to the thing. The Flamen Dialis was forbidden to touch a dog, or a goat, raw flesh, ivy, or beans. He was forbidden also even to name them. The harm that might come through them could also be communicated through their names.[1]

Mr. Grant Allen speaks of touch as "the mother tongue of the affections." It would be difficult to exaggerate the importance of this sense for the emotions. We find evidence of this in the way in which touch was used to interpret the influence of one being or object upon another. The kingly virtue was thought in England until quite recently to pass at the royal contact into those afflicted with "the king's evil." It is still believed by many that the touch of the mesmerist conveys some strange influence into the body of his patient. From this point of view we can interpret many regulations observed in Rome. Women were thought to be possessed of very perilous properties. If these passed into the food of the citizens, there was no knowing what might happen. Women were not permitted, therefore, in ancient times, to grind the corn, or to dress the meat in the kitchen. Hence too, on the other hand, the Flamen Dialis, whose life seems to have been thought of as bound up in a special way with the public welfare, was forbidden to touch many

[1] Plut. *R. Q.* 111.

things, lest apparently evil influences should pass from them to him.[1]

In this way the being of everything was, so to speak, spread out. It ran into every object with which it had been in contact. This was specially true of persons. Whatever has belonged to a man at any time is still a part of him, and he can be influenced through it. They used to tell us, when we were children, that when a tooth was drawn it ought to be thrown, along with some salt, into the fire. Else when the angel of the resurrection came, we should have to wander until we found it. For if it got into the wrong hands, there was no knowing what might happen. In the same spirit, the Roman witches used to draw back their truant lovers through their relics—a lock of hair, or some article of attire which they might have left behind them. In the Isle of Man, if one fisherman is on bad terms with another, he will pluck a straw from the other's dwelling, as he goes past in the morning, and his victim, having thus lost his luck, will catch no fish that day.

Let us follow out this idea a little further. When the same thing is applied to a large number of persons in common, it will constitute a kind of bond among them. Blood or fat seem to have been regarded, as in special senses, the vehicles of life. Hence the application of them on public occasions

[1] Plut. *R. Q.* 85, 111.

brought the persons to whom they were applied into the charmed circle of the communal existence. We shall have a future opportunity of developing some further consequences of this idea.

The bride, on entering her new home, smeared the doorposts with swine's fat. This is explained when we find that it was an ancient custom in Italy for the newly-wedded pair to sacrifice a pig.[1] The life of the pig was thus applied to the home of those who had already partaken of it together in sacrifice. We have already seen how, at the Lupercalia, the youths who ran through the streets had their faces smeared with blood from the victim. They were thus made one with it. Hence, as they struck at the passers-by with goatskin, they enabled them to share in the virtues of the offering. The application of the blood to the faces of the youths, and the blows with the leather strips, were two stages in this process. When the blood or the fat of the victim was applied to the face of the god, or of his human representative, the oneness of the community with the object of its worship was signified and *produced*. In the worship of Bellona, the priests used to make incisions into their shoulders, and carry drawn swords, with the blades laid on their hands. Their blood was sprinkled upon the image of the deity, and used in the sacrifice.[2]

---

[1] Plin. *N. H.* xxviii. 135. Varro, *R. R.* ii. 10.
[2] *Rel. Sem.* 304. Lact. i. 21.

Other red substances might be used as substitutes. On solemn occasions the images of the gods were painted with vermilion; in the same way, as to this day, the Hindus smear the monkey-god Hanuman. One of the first duties of the newly-appointed censors was to have the great statue of Jupiter on the Capitol so treated. The country people honoured the rustic gods in the same way. Not only was minium so applied to the gods, it was daubed also over the persons of the generals who celebrated a triumph. For they were regarded as the representatives of the deity. The rustic worshipper often followed the same habit.[1] The feeling that minium possessed a certain sanctity seems to have led to its use upon funeral inscriptions, and also to mark out the more important passages in documents. These usages are very widely spread. The Khonds used to bedaub themselves with red at their human sacrifices. The victim, however, was anointed with oil and melted butter, and was also painted with saffron. They also smear with saffron the stone which represents the Great Father. So, too, just before the Roman Brethren of the Field closed the temple doors for their solemn hymn, they anointed the effigies of the goddesses with oil, doubtless taken from one of the victims. We are reminded of the anointing which played so large a part in Jewish ritual. Jacob's pillar was anointed in the same way as the images of the

[1] Plut. *R. Q.* 98. Plin. *N. H.* xxxiii. 111. Tib. II. i. 55.

goddesses, and the doorposts of the new Roman home.[1]

Among the questions which Plutarch set himself to answer about Roman customs, we find this, "Why is it that all other offerings to the gods have reverence done to them, and receive repairs when they require them, while the spoils taken in war are allowed to perish in lapse of time?" This was probably permitted in order that the enemy to whom they had belonged might perish in like manner. Here we light upon another principle of the First Philosophy. *Effects are like their causes.* When the tables were taken away after a Roman banquet something was left upon them. This made certain a continual supply for the future. On the other hand, it was very unlucky if the floor was swept as anyone rose from a meal; as also if a table or a tray was removed while anyone was drinking. The one who left the company ran the risk of being swept out of existence; and the drinker, of never drinking again. You were not to rise before the feast was over, lest your rising brought about your departure from the feast of life. It was of bad omen for a dish to be removed untasted, or for anyone to sit at the meal without eating at all. If a morsel fell from the hand, it was put back upon the table. You were forbidden to blow the crumbs away. If in any mistaken zeal for neatness

[1] Reclus, *Prim. Folk*, 303, 311. Wilm. 2879. *Rel. Sem.* 187.

this had been done, the fragments had to be picked up, put on the table, and burnt to the house spirit. The modern custom of leaving a few ears of corn in the field for the gleaners is a survival from a similar circle of beliefs.[1]

The Flamen Dialis must go as free as possible, lest through him the city should become crippled. He might not use a knot in his girdle or headgear, or in any other part of his attire. He was prohibited from wearing a ring unless it was first broken. If anyone came into the residence of the Flamen in fetters he had to be released. In such a case the chains were drawn up through the opening of the court of the house, and thrown over the tiles into the street. They might not be carried over the sacred threshold.[2]

In Sweden no spinning is done on Thursday night, for fear of offending the spirit who watches over the cattle and the crops. The twisting of the thread and the downward pull of the spindle might affect the growth of the corn. This is the way, perhaps, in which we may interpret a rule of which Pliny speaks. Women passing along a country road might not twist their spindles or even leave them uncovered, as this was very harmful for all crops, especially of corn.[3]

---

[1] Plut. *R. Q.* 37. Plin. *N. H.* xxviii. 26, 27.
[2] Gell. *N. A.* x. 15.
[3] Mannhardt, *A. F. W.* i. 60. Plin. *N. H.* xxviii. 28.

We find these ideas carried out with great consistency in the law of Rome. The actions which were employed, imitated the effects which, from time to time, the lawyers had in view, and the objects with which such actions were conversant, represented, directly or indirectly, what was at stake. " Persons, slave and free, and likewise animals that are things mancipable, cannot be mancipated unless they are present, and so strictly is this the case, that it is necessary for him who takes the thing by mancipation to grasp that which is given to him; whence the term mancipation is derived, because the thing is taken by the hand." Thus contact is necessary in this most ancient form of sale, in order that the new ownership might be established. And although an estate could be mancipated at a distance, still a sod, a brick, or a tile, must be brought to be handled. These acts were more than symbolic. They produced, it was thought, the new condition of ownership. The handling of the sod is equivalent in these ancient modes of thought to laying hold upon the stretch of land from which it was taken. Hence any error of procedure was more than formal. It rendered of no avail the whole series of acts; if, for example, the purchaser omitted to take the sod of earth, or if it were not taken from the land in question. So in the consecration of a temple the priest laid his hand upon the doorpost.

Again, if the words of the contracting parties were

thought to have magical power, we can perceive why an error in the expression employed made null the effect to be obtained by their means. How real this belief was, appears from many instances. A building had been unduly consecrated. The Senate charged the praetor to see to it that it did not retain a sacred character, and especially that all letters incised upon its materials should be removed; as though they would otherwise go on "raining influence."[1] When the Romans were digging out foundations on the Tarpeian rock, they found a human head. Envoys were sent by the Senate into Etruria to enquire about the matter, and a very famous seer, Olenus of Cales, seeing the brilliant fortune presaged by the discovery, tried to turn it to the benefit of his own nation. He drew on the ground a sketch of the site with his stick, and asked, "Do you say, men of Rome, *this is to be the temple of Jupiter Greatest and Best; here we found the head?*" The annals are agreed that the Roman destiny would have passed over to Etruria, unless the envoys had been warned by the son of the seer. They replied, "It is not here but at Rome that we say the head was found." From this and similar stories we can appreciate the strictness demanded by the Romans in the recitation of legal formulae.[2]

According to primitive thought, events which occur

---

[1] Gaius, i. 121. Cic. *de Domo sua*, 137.
[2] Plin. *N. H.* xxviii. 15.

together or in immediate succession are connected as cause and effect. We need not ever look very far back for the cause of a thing. Some incident of the moment which attracts the popular eye, will explain the whole issue of a great and complex crisis. The Etruscans set definite limits to the prophetic influence of omens. The fortunes of individuals were not indicated more than ten years ahead, while the destiny of the State loomed over it as far forward as thirty years.[1] But these limits pass those set by the lay mind. It loved to dwell most upon coincidences. By observing these it appeared that certain occurrences were associated with good fortune, others with ill fortune. It will not surprise us that among these occurrences an important place is given to the words that happen to be uttered. The good wishes to which the Romans gave expression on the morning of the new year, were more than mere sounds to them; they were means operating towards the happiness of the next twelvemonths. A like feeling led them to choose names of good omen for the attendants who led the victims at the public purifications. Closely connected with the belief that words bring luck or bad fortune, is the belief that numbers influence the course of things. "We believe," says Pliny, "that odd numbers have more power than even ones." "God takes delight in odd numbers,"

---

[1] Plin. *N. H.* ii. 139.

says Virgil.[1] Even numbers were less lucky. The Calends, Nones, and Ides, of the Roman month were always so arranged as to fall upon odd days; whereas the days that immediately followed them were unlucky. On these latter the Romans refused to begin a journey, and the army never took the field. Five wax candles, neither more nor less, were lighted at weddings. Names are repeated quite superfluously in curses that the mystical number three may be reached. The power of the charm against gout obviously depended upon its being repeated nine times.[2]

We may suppose that many beliefs as to the lucky or unlucky character of actions or things arose from coincidences. A single one, if it were striking, would be able to establish a custom. We may refer to this source some customs at least. It was best, for instance, to put the right foot foremost. The steps in front of temples were of unequal number, in order that the worshipper, beginning to ascend with the right foot, might set the same foot on the top step. The Moslem still puts his right foot first over the threshold on entering a mosque.[3]

The belief in the evil eye accounted for the fact that some persons brought ill luck. If a misfortune seemed to be connected with the approach

---

[1] Plin. *N. H.* xxviii. 23. Virg. *Ecl.* viii. 76.

[2] Plut. *R. Q.* 2, 25. Wilm. 2747.

[3] Vitr. iii. 4, 4.

of anyone, it was because he had the fatal gift. Those who have read Gautier's striking story, *Jettatura*, will realise the strength of the superstition in antiquity. The numerous charms and amulets that have been found show that in this, as in other respects, the great Roman writers give a very imperfect picture of their contemporaries.

It is a fitting conclusion to this enumeration of Roman modes of thought, that we should turn for a moment to the belief in metamorphoses. Anything could become anything else. We shall find in the next chapter that this belief underlies many magical practices. It is the necessary corollary of the inability to conceive of the order of Nature as fixed and determinate. Ovid, in his poem, *The Metamorphoses*, has described in great detail a large series of human beings who changed their form ; but his material is drawn almost wholly from Greek sources, and does not represent genuine Italian tradition.

ROMAN MAGIC

THERE is no more melancholy chapter in the history of the human race than that which deals with witchcraft and its punishment. As late as 1736, the statute book of this country contained laws against witchcraft. Nor had they long been a dead letter. In 1722, a so-called witch was done to death by process of law in Sutherlandshire.[1] Cotton Mather, in New England, and Richard Baxter, on this side of the Atlantic, did all they could, a generation before that time, to rouse the blind fury of popular prejudice. An old Frenchman was drowned in Essex, on suspicion of sorcery, so late as 1863.[2] It is doubtful whether, in the middle ages, as many persons lost their lives in the cause of religion by the executioner, as were harried out of this world, with the applause of all parties, on the charge of witchcraft. When the services of the modern scientific movement are reckoned up, this should be included as one of the greatest; that it has done something to free mankind from this

---

[1] Tuke, *History of the Insane in the British Isles*, 39.
[2] Lyall, *Asiatic Studies*, 11.

loathsome bondage of belief in sorcery. It is likely that this one superstition has led in Europe to the judicial murder of at least half a million persons, and these, in great part, unoffending lonely old women.

We seem to breathe an air more like that of the present, as we turn from the middle ages to a writer of the first century. "The art of magic," says Pliny the elder, "has prevailed in most ages and in most parts of the globe." (This assertion might have been made to include the future as well.) "Let no one," proceeds Pliny, "wonder that it has wielded very great authority, inasmuch as it embraces three other sources of influence. No one doubts that it took its rise in medicine, and sought to cloak itself in the garb of a science more profound and holy than the common run. It added to its tempting promises the force of religion, after which the human race is groping, especially at this time. Further, it has brought in the arts of astrology and divination. For everyone desires to know what is to come to him, and believes that certainty can be gained by consulting the stars. Having in this way taken captive the feelings of man by a triple chain, it has reached such a pitch that it rules over all the world, and, in the East, governs the kings of kings." Pliny is mistaken in supposing that all the practices with which we are about to deal took their rise in purposive invention. But he is nearer the truth when he brings magic into connection with medicine, divination, and worship. It will be our business to trace out the mode in which this relation should be viewed.

At first the observances of religion were practical expedients, directed towards given ends. Only by degrees did they gain that ethical and spiritual meaning which, in Western countries, is now their distinguishing feature. We might even define religion, in the most primitive form in which it presents itself, as *magic employed for public ends*. A few illustrations will make this clear.

A stone used to be kept in a temple of Mars, just outside the gates of Rome. Whenever there was a drought, it used to be brought by the pontiffs into the city. Immediately the rain came down in showers.[1] Another artifice of state magic is to be seen in the throwing of puppets into the Tiber, which took place every May. This seems to have been also a rain charm.[2] "At Bucharest, the trial has taken place of two boys, aged six and fourteen respectively, who confessed that they had drowned deliberately a child two years old. They declared that the long drought and total lack of rain had to be put a stop to by some means. This extraordinary defence is explained by an old custom of the country. The children of the villages, in times of great drought, are made to throw a clay figure

[1] Preller, *Röm. Myth.* i. 354.
[2] Mannhardt, *A. F. W.* i. 265 ff.

of a child into the water. The boys drowned the child merely because they had no clay figure. The elder was sentenced to two years' imprisonment."[1] Thus the customs of the Roumanians of the present enable us to enter into the mind of the Roman officers of religion two thousand years ago. But there is no need to go as far away as this for parallels. At Loddiswell, near Plymouth, Mayday is known as *ducking day*, it being the custom for the boys, whenever they have the chance, to throw water over the passers-by. In May of last year (1894), this custom was carried out as a conveyance was approaching. The horses ran away, and the occupant was thrown out and killed. The name "ducking day" points to a practice similar to the Roumanian one.[2]

It may be questioned whether the average man is ever quite at ease in a thunderstorm. The Emperor Tiberius used to be scared out of his wits by one; when the sky was threatening, he went about with a laurel wreath on his head, because that kind of foliage was said to be proof against lightning. Augustus took measures still more elaborate. He carried a sealskin about with him always and everywhere. When there was the least suspicion of a storm, he used to put this on and go down into the cellar. A similar practice to that of Tiberius

---

[1] *Nottm. Evening News*, Dec. 6, 1894.

[2] *Nottm. Evening Post*, May 18, 1894.

is found in Germany to-day. In the Black Forest poles are erected, with bouquets at the top, to keep off the lightning. We may appreciate the importance of the charm which the priests had at their disposal at Rome, when we learn that it was disclosed to them by the god of thunder. In making use of it, as in trundling the *lapis manalis* along into the city, they were performing acts which directly produce results beneficial to the community.[1]

The State magic of Rome culminates in the use of the *indigitamenta*. We have seen that they contained the names of those spirits who guard each single action with which man is concerned. In the thought of a Roman, the name of a spirit was strong enough, if uttered, to evoke him. Thus the pontiffs who had charge of these lists were enabled to call forth just those influences which were demanded by each particular occasion. The sacred formulae which we find here and there were derived from their suggestion. When Decius devoted himself to death for the victory of the Roman forces, he invoked a long series of gods—Janus, Jupiter, Father Mars, Quirinus, Bellona, the Lares, the new gods, the gods who were on the sacred list, *indigites*, the gods who have power over our countrymen and the enemy, the deified dead, *dii manes*.[2] This all-embracing list answers to the interests at stake. In less important

---

[1] Suet. *Aug.* 90; *Tib.* 69. Baring-Gould, *Strange Survivals*, 52.
[2] Liv. viii. 9.

cases, one or two special spirits were summoned. All instances exhibit to us the careful Roman, taking every precaution lest any deity should be omitted whose assistance was desirable, and also his strong belief in the efficacy of invocations, when they were rightly performed.

The primitive theory of disease does not admit that it can arise in the natural order of things. It is due to the anger of some spirit, or the machinations of some enemy. In Juvenal's time, an ailing Roman, who was racked with pain and fever, thought that his disease was sent by an offended deity. Hence a cure seemed possible, if the deity in question could be appeased by sacrifice and prayer. In such terms, perhaps, we might express the feelings of a man whose religion had risen above the primitive belief in magic. If, however, we turn to the methods that were actually resorted to by the early Roman, they are at once seen to be of the same kind with other magical expedients. The elder Cato gives a formula which was potent against sprains—*havat havat havat ista pista sista damia bodanna ustra*—which was, in all likelihood, no better understood by the Romans than by us. He thought that sleeplessness might be cured by eating hare. Where the expedients of popular medicine are not trivial, they are characterised as a rule by their offensive character. We turn with relief from them to the graceful idea, borrowed from Greece, that the cure of disease was disclosed by the god of healing to his worshipper in dreams. The philosophic emperor, Marcus Aurelius, records with gratitude the relief that had been vouchsafed to him by this means. When disease ceased to be confined to individuals, and became epidemic, it was the duty of the religious officials of the state to find a cure of corresponding scope. On one occasion the matrons of Rome swept with their hair the temple floors. The plague ceased thereupon. Livy, however, is uncertain whether the cessation ought to be attributed to the "peace of the gods," which was so obtained, or to the more favourable season of the year.[1]

If it appears from this that the medicine of the Romans was in about the same stage of advancement as, say, in the time of Shakespeare, we must give them credit for dealing with the phenomena of insanity in a manner more consonant with common sense, than the treatment which was meted out to the insane during the whole of the middle ages. Although there are indications that madness was viewed by the common people as a kind of possession by spirits, this belief did not govern the attitude of the Roman lawyers. The person of disordered mind was not deprived of the control of his estate, unless he turned out to be entirely incapable. When this was the case he was put

---

[1] Cato, *R. R.* 160. Plin. *N. H.* xxviii. 260. Antonin. *Medit.* i. 17, ix. 27. Liv. iii. 7.

under the guardianship of his nearest kinsman. His guardian was bound to keep him both from injuring himself and others. In fact, insanity was treated as "a sickness and disease of the mind," to use Cicero's phrase. There is a curious piece of evidence, by which we may infer that the lot of the insane was a mild one at Rome. It became actually a practice for citizens to feign madness, that they might have a guardian assigned to them, and thus shirk public duty. If they had lived as late as the seventeenth century, they would have hesitated to feign lunacy; for they would have run the risk of being burnt as witches and as possessed with devils.

A rescript of the Emperor Marcus Aurelius deals with insanity in its relation to crime. One Aelius Priscus had murdered his mother, and the plea of insanity was set up. The emperor wrote that if his madness was of such a character that he was devoid of reason through the uninterrupted derangement of his mind, he was not to be punished; his insanity being in itself sufficient penalty. He was, however, to be kept in more strict watch, and, if it should seem good to the magistrate, to be put in chains for the safety of his neighbours. Inquiry was ordered to be made whether reasonable precautions were taken by his relatives. The annals of medical jurisprudence show how late modern Europe has been in arriving even at this stage of enlightenment.[1]

[1] *Dig.* i. 17, 14; xxvii. 10, 6. Cic. *Tusc.* iii. 8.

In the minds of the mediaeval judges, superstitious dread of witchcraft, and the belief in demoniacal possession, combined to blind them to the true nature of insanity. "It is indeed impossible," says Dr. Tuke, "to read the narratives of some of the unfortunate hags who were put to death for witchcraft, without recognising the well-marked features of the victims of cerebral disease. In this way I have no doubt that a considerable number of mad people were destroyed."[1] Perhaps these considerations will enable us to understand why the Romans escaped the awful stain which lies across the whole page of modern history. In this respect we must set their intellectual advancement very high indeed.

The origin of most of the usages included under the head of magic is enveloped in darkness. We can, however, trace some to their source. When the early Romans passed from their own soil to that of strangers, it was with hesitation and dread. In their own land, every familiar spot seemed to be hallowed by the remains of their dead, or the presence of some guardian spirit. It was far otherwise elsewhere. A foreign land was haunted by spirits in sympathy with, or under the control of, enemies. And the nation who dwelt in it seemed to wield powers of an unusual kind. The Marsi, who inhabited the central highlands to the east of Rome, were believed to be a nation of wizards.

[1] *Op. cit.* p. 36.

L

They were said to have sprung from a son of the enchantress Circe, by a legend invented to explain a feeling which already existed in the popular mind. Further, their bodies had a natural virtue, whereby they resisted the poison of serpents.[1] Thus fear and dislike of the foreign race is combined with belief in their magical powers. Hence, also, when a primitive people migrates into the land of another, it brings with it a feeling towards the original occupants, which manifests itself in many ways. Let us trace the bearing of this on Roman beliefs and practices.

The great temple of Jupiter, rising on the southern knoll of the Capitoline Hill, was the centre of Roman worship. Other deities also were honoured in the same sanctuary with Jove Best and Mightiest. He occupied the nave, but the eastern aisle was consecrated to Minerva, the western to Juno. The composite character of this chief seat of Roman worship bears witness to the mingling of the stocks that worshipped there. But another and more primitive deity kept his place with these three. At the foundation of the temple, many of the small chapels which clustered together on this " high place " were desecrated in order to make room for the new-comers. But the boundary spirit Terminus refused, it was said, to depart, and his chapel was included in the temple precincts. Mr. Gomme has suggested

[1] Plin. *N. H.* vii. 15.

that stone worship among Aryan races was taken over from the vanquished non-Aryans, among whom they lived as their lords.[2] We may suppose that the stone which represented Terminus was a relic from the original dwellers by the Tiber. Roman traditions and rites point to the existence of a people with whom the Romans mingled, as strangers coming from without. The savage nature of many of the Roman customs may be due, therefore—in part, at least—to borrowing from less civilised neighbours. In India the non-Aryan races are credited with supernatural powers by their more cultured neighbours, who join in their rites at fixed seasons, although at other times they disdain commerce with them. In applying this analogy to Rome, we seem to meet a case in which the contrast of superior and inferior is less strongly marked.[2]

We may expect, therefore, to find parallels among savage races of the present, for some of the usages which, perhaps, the Romans borrowed. The smearing of the face with the blood of the victim at the Lupercalia suggests that the Luperci once rent the goat with their teeth, like the priest in the festival of the village goddess in some parts of Southern India. So also the smearing of the body of the triumphant general, or of the rustic worshipper, seems to be paralleled by the usage of the Damaras, who smear the bodies

---

[1] *Ethnology in Folk Lore*, 19.
[2] Liv. i. 2.

of the messengers sent into the lands of foreign tribes; or of the Donagla, among whom the bridegroom is anointed from head to foot on the afternoon preceding the wedding day.[2]

The flint which plays so large and so strange a part in the worship of Jove may be related to the use of flint by the aborigines. The evil spirits appear as stone-age men, "shy of their conquerors, and loathing their agriculture."[2] Tokens of husbandry were a charm against the wild men of the woods.

If the primitive inhabitants of the district were not acquainted with the use of iron, it may well have been thought to exercise some influence hostile to them. And since the superior race thought of them as specially leagued with evil spirits, the iron which was hostile to them would also ward off their familiars. Hence the Flamen Dialis slept with iron at the head of his bed, as a preservative against them. The bridge of piles over the Tiber was apparently of very ancient date. If it was first built before the use of iron was brought in, it is clear why this metal was not permitted to be used in repairs in later times. The taboo of iron was extended to typical Roman usages. It would be interesting to know why an axe might not be used on the wood of the funeral pyre. Was it because

---

[1] Gomme, *op. cit.* 25. Casati, *Ten Years in Equatoria*, i. 69.
[2] cf. Tylor, *Prim. Cult.* i 386.

the iron would scare away the spirit of the dead man, and cause him to haunt the streets, instead of resting peacefully with his ashes ?[1]

There is some justification, therefore, for attributing, in part at least, the use of magical rites to the influence of the neighbours of the Romans. Some of these rites were borrowed directly, others arose out of the relation of the newcomers to the original inhabitants. In historical times the beliefs of the Roman continued to be influenced largely by his immediate neighbours. And with the new beliefs he adopted related practices. The Etruscans indeed determined the development of his art of prophecy, rather than the cruder usages of his magic; we shall have occasion afterwards to observe this point more closely. But it is to the Greeks and the peoples further east, that we must look chiefly for the origin of the rites that rose to such prominence in the later years of the Republic.

(How was it that the Romans were so ready to adopt foreign usages? / The answer is to be found in the formal character of their religion. Each act was directed to some practical end, and expressed nothing more than the expectancy of a certain result. The Romans were rich in the things of the world of practice, in subordination to authority, in rigorous self-direction to the matter in hand, in unconquered perseverance. They were poor in

[1] Gell. *N. A.* x. 15. *xii. Tab.* 9.

imagination and the gifts upon which it rests, in sympathy, insight, and a love of ideal satisfactions. They were "cumbered with much serving," and found it difficult to employ in a reasonable manner the leisure which came in the train of their successes. Their ideas were like the shadows which take colour from surrounding objects. Hence, instead of clinging like nations of higher spiritual endowment, the Jews for instance, all the more closely to their ritual in times of depression, they had recourse continually to fresh objects of veneration: not for the sake of the new deities, but because they hoped that the new charms would be more efficacious than the old ones they discarded. Nor in surrendering the old did they seem to have lost any dear and familiar consolation.

The attitude which the Romans as a nation thus adopted is carried out in their private life with great consistency. The individual for whom the State magic ceased to be more than a matter of form, had recourse to foreign wizards. In fact, the Government followed popular feeling at a distance in admitting new observances. We might be quite sure that for each new worship received formally into the State, there were a dozen others taken up by the citizens in their private capacity.

It has been well said that some magic is a kind of private religion. The individual attempts to employ for his own benefit other, and as he conceives, more powerful agencies than those provided in public ordinances. Hence in most ancient states the use of magic was viewed with great suspicion. In Palestine witchcraft was punishable with death. At Rome, however, there was so great an analogy between the State religion and the practice of private magic, that the latter was left undisturbed as a rule.

When magic is thus described to consist in borrowing from foreign religions, it is not meant, of course, that the whole of the foreign religion was borrowed. The loan was of a very limited character. It simply consisted in those elements which could be taken over by a people with the temper of the primitive Roman, namely, in the imitation of certain definite acts. Since the Roman attached little emotional signification to his national ritual, it was not to be expected that he should do more for the ritual of another race. We are thus brought back to the account of magic with which we started, special acts performed with a view to some practical end. When the emotional life of Rome was enriched by the admixture of other civilisations, this mechanical form of borrowing was no longer possible. Foreign religions were better understood. Magic was discredited in its grosser forms. Instead of coming in partially as magic, external faiths were introduced under the form of mysteries.

At the same time there is a magical element in the mysteries which must not be overlooked. The ritual of the devotees of Isis impressed the Roman by its strangeness. He hoped to find in it a strength which the more familiar usages of his own worship appeared to have lost.

Further, the peculiar character which the mysteries possessed in the eyes of the ancient world, was largely due to their private nature. Just as magic consisted, so to speak, in wonder-working formulae unknown to the world in general, so the devotee of any mysteries was lifted away into a new world, and this not of action alone, but of feeling and belief. In fact, the distinction between the initiated and the profane could only arise in the presence of strangers. So that we hear of mysteries in two cases: when worships are transplanted to a foreign soil, and when they are resorted to by strangers. The mysteries of Isis, in their Roman shape, are a good instance of the former; those of Demeter at Eleusis of the latter. And even the native worships gain somewhat of the same tinge. For all ancient worship was in some measure an initiation into a society. Hence, when a stranger came in contact with it, he had to undergo at once experiences that for a regular worshipper might be spread over a term of years. The minute rules, which the new-comer was instructed to observe, were viewed in the light of the solemn company which he was invited to join, and so were lifted above the mere magic of traditional acts. And so it could be that religions like that of Egypt, which were in some respects as coarse as savage religions, gained a sanctity at Rome which was not without a good effect upon the lives of their devotees.

The lower kind of borrowing went on by the side of the higher; foreign magic continued to come in as well as foreign mysteries. Horace has described for us with some detail, the antics of two witches in the old cemetery of the Esquiline. They steal into it as soon as it is the new moon, to pick up bones and noxious herbs. They come along barefoot, with their hair flowing and their robes tucked up. They alarm the neighbours with their cries. A hollow is made in the ground with their nails, and as they rend a black lamb piecemeal with their teeth, its bloc. drops into it. As the ghosts of the dead come to this ghastly banquet, they are questioned by the beldames. Then they take two images. One of wool stands for one of the witches. The other, of wax, is for the man whom she wishes to punish for his falseness. In mystical gestures she indicates the torture which is to befal him. As they pray to the powers of hell, infernal hounds and snakes glide over the spot. The very moon turns red. Since the muzzle of a wolf acted as a counter charm against witches (it was often nailed upon the gates of country houses, like our horse-shoes), they proceed to bury one away. Then they set about burning the image of wax. As it melts away, the man for whom it stands, melts out of life, like him on whom Sister Helen exercised her arts. It was believed upon the death of Germanicus, that in like manner he had been the victim of Piso. His name was found written upon tablets of lead, together with curses, by which he was consigned to the infernal gods.[1]

Magical arts were also used in the service of tenderer feelings. The witch who was practising upon the love of a youth, would make an effigy of him. This she bound with threads of divers colours, and carried it thrice round an altar. By this means he was entangled in his passion. Next she put clay and wax and bay leaves into the fire. As the clay grew firm, the wax melted, and the laurel burned in the flame, so Daphnis' love would endure, his heart melt, and he himself burn with love. There is a prescription in a sixteenth century manuscript at Nuremberg, *ad amorem in mulieribus*. By burning a rue plant with various precautions, the affection of any given lady might be secured. As the rue burnt in the embers, so her heart was to be kindled.[2]

When we bring the principles that we have already traced in early thought to bear upon these practices, their meaning becomes clear. The witches relied in the main upon the efficacy of imitation; they were Symbolists. For them likeness of gesture, or of form, did more than foreshadow; it actually

---

[1] Tac. *Ann.* ii. 69; *supra*, p. 40.
[2] Virg. *Eclog.* viii. 74. *Rhein. Mus.* xlix. 43.

brought about what they intended. So, at least they seem to have thought. Although they never raised their concrete concepts to the purity of the idea, we may perhaps be allowed to do this for them. They would doubtless have admitted also, if questioned, that they gave a very broad interpretation to the principle of identity. It was enough for them if they could gain possession of a lock of hair, or some article of wear, to get anybody entirely into their power. Through that part of the individual in question (for is it not clear that what we have possessed at any time becomes a part of us?), they could do with him what they liked.

When they came to the written or spoken word, their contemporaries were not less impressed by their resources. As they muttered in the lonely cemeteries, one was filled with alarm. Were they going to draw down the moon out of heaven? It was believed that they had the power. Hey presto! And it was done—*if, that is, the witch knew just the right formula.*[1] They had hosts of servants under their control. You might hear them questioning the dead, and getting their replies in the squeaky yet stern accents of the dwellers by Acheron's banks. In their more appalling moments the wizards rose even to higher flights than their sisters. They claimed to dispose of the whole realm of spirits in the name of the Supreme Being. "I am BARBARADONAI," says

[1] Prop. I. i. 19.

an enchanter, "who conceals the stars, the shining lord of heaven, the master of the universe."[1]   In New York there is a negro drug-seller, who has the name of being the most successful wizard in that abode of success.   Like his Greek brother, he speaks in the name of "the Great Sovereign of the Universe."

[1] *Rhein. Mus.* xlix. 52.

DIVINATION AND PROPHECY

MAGIC, as it dies away, passes through the intermediate stage of divination. The wizard was credited at one time with the power of governing the future. When his claims were no longer admitted, it was still thought that he could forecast what was to come. If special sources of power no longer were accessible, at least—so the fancy ran—there were secret channels through which indications of the future might reach mankind. The religion of the Roman State exhibits this transition to us very clearly. We just catch traces in it of that early time in which it was wonder-working. For the most part, however, it has already passed, in historical times, to its later form. It interprets the divine will by the tokens that are disclosed to the officers of the State. Thunder, the cries and flight of birds, the entrails of the sacrificial victim, these foreshadow what is to come, to eyes that have been trained in accordance with ancestral precedents. Here again we shall find the closest fellow-feeling between the religion of the State and of the individual. Hence it will be possible to blend in one account the beliefs and practices of both governors and governed.

Divination was reduced to a science by the Stoics. Cicero borrows wholesale from them in the account that he gives of it in the first book *De Divinatione*. It is noteworthy how far the show of system goes in commending the most fanciful and absurd statements to a certain class of minds. Many of Cicero's contemporaries, and among them his brother Quintus, repeated with great edification the lessons they had received from their Greek friends. Divination, we are assured, is of two kinds.[1] It may proceed by system, or without system; it is *artificial* or *natural*. On the one hand, we make use of the symbols to which the observation of antiquity has attached a meaning. The behaviour of birds, the appearance of the intestines of the sacred ox or sheep; from such hints as these we can infer what is about to happen. On the other hand, there are those who have presentiments of the future in the troubling of their spirit, when it seems to move in freedom from its entanglements. This happens to mankind generally in dreams, and also to those who prophesy when they are in a state of frenzy.

This distinction will be useful to us still. We shall find it advantageous to treat first of what the Stoics called natural divination. In taking leave of the Roman witches, we noticed the supremacy

[1] Cic. *Div.* i. 34.

they were believed to exercise over spirits, and of the dead in particular. Magic was referred to the operation of spirits. The same agencies were believed to bring certain knowledge to the dreamer. Near Laurentum was a spot called Albunea. Here a sulphur spring welled up in the middle of a great wood. It was resorted to by all the country round. The worshipper offered sacrifice, and slept on the skins of the victims. In his slumbers he heard strange voices, and enjoyed the converse of the gods; while before his eyes there flitted the strange phantoms of souls.

At other times the human body was occupied by a foreign spirit. The seer was filled with heaven, and celestial influences. His stature was increased, and a certain majesty was poured upon him; *Deus inclusus corpore humano*—" God dwelling in a human body"—says Cicero. And the words that fell from the lips of the prophet seemed to be dictated by the gods. Rome had not to go back to legendary times for these inspired utterances. In the middle of the second war with Carthage, there were published two prophecies of Marcius, and Livy is enabled to furnish us with specimens of them. Cicero speaks of prophecies attributed to another seer, Publicius, and also of mysteries of Apollo, as being current in his time.[1]

Utterances of this kind were thought to have a

---

[1] *Supra*, p. 42. Virg. *Aen.* vii. 83. Livy, xxv. 12. Cic. *Div.* ii. 113.

permanent value. They were collected, and consulted in times of perplexity. The most famous of these collections was attributed to the Sibyl of Cumae, one of those majestic figures who overshadow the simple singing-maidens of the country. In heroic times, Aeneas is represented as promising to the priestess of Cumae to found that sacred college which was entrusted with the Sibylline books. In the time of the later monarchy, her successor—so the legend ran—offered her collection in nine books to King Tarquinius Priscus for £300. The king thought the price was exorbitant. Thereupon she burnt three of the books, and still demanded the same amount. Again he refused to buy, and again she burnt three more of the books. The king became alarmed, and agreed to pay the full price for the remaining three. " It seems probable," says Mr. Paley, "that these far-famed books were—in part, at least—the prophets of the Old Testament." He found reason for believing also that the burnt volumes contained the least valuable part of the whole. It must be said, however, that no reasons of weight can be alleged in favour of Mr. Paley's fanciful assumption. The three sacred books were entrusted at first to two guardians; a number increased to ten in 367 B.C., and to fifteen in the time of Sulla. They held their office for life, and were exempt from all military and civil obligations. The books were kept in the crypt of the great Capitoline Temple, and were preserved there until the conflagration of 83 B.C. " The oracles which are now extant," says Dionysius, " have been brought together from various places; some from the cities of Italy: others from Erythrae, in Asia, envoys being sent to transcribe them, by order of the senate. Others again were written down by private individuals, among which are many spurious ones. These may be detected by their acrostic character."[1] Out of those which were so selected, the pontiffs put together about a thousand lines in all. The partisans of Caesar produced some verses in acrostics, which were professedly Sibylline. These enjoined on the Romans to make him king in name who was already king in deed, if they wished to be safe. Cicero speaks of them as obvious forgeries. When Augustus became chief pontiff, he made a fresh recension of all the floating prophetic writings which were current, to the number of two thousand, in his time; he retained those only which were manifestly Sibylline in character. These he put in two cases, under the great Palatine statue of that Apollo under whose inspiration the mysterious verses were spoken. In the year 32 A.D., one of the college of fifteen, Caninius Gallus, thought that a book which went by the name of the Sibyl should be added to the sacred collection. A motion to this effect was carried in the senate. Tiberius thereupon sent down a message, and blamed the procedure adopted. The

---

[1] *Fasti*, iv. 257.   D. II. iv. 62.

sacred college included five "masters" in its numbers, and the duty was theirs, rather than of the Senate, to read and estimate the hymns offered for insertion.

The hymns of all the Sibyls were extant in the time of Lactantius. The sayings attributed to the Erythraean Sibyl include some striking statements of monotheistic belief. But the line in the famous fourth eclogue of Virgil:

The last times foretold in the song of Cumae are at hand,

established the authority of the Cumaean Sibyl in the early Church. The Sibylline books recognised the division of time into ages in a manner that appealed to men who lived in expectation of the end of the world. In the solemn hymn which is sung at the mass for the dead, the Sibyl is joined with David as witness to that day of wrath which shall bring time to a close amid fire and ashes. Augustine was once conversing with a friend of high rank, who produced a Greek book, which, he said, contained the hymns of the Erythraean Sibyl. He pointed out an acrostic which contained apparently the name of Christ. Augustine, after quoting it, says that the sibyl must be regarded as of those who belong to the kingdom of God.[1]

In this respect, at least, the Christian religion was represented as gathering up into itself the nobler

---

[1] Tac. *Ann.* vi. 12.   Lact. *Inst.* i. 6.   Aug. *Civ. Dei*, xviii. 23.

aspirations of paganism, rather than as opposed to it, root and branch.

There is a curious story, which reminds the reader somewhat of the finding of the law in the time of Josiah. In the year 181 B.C., some farm labourers were at work on the land of a public notary. They came across two stone chests, about eight feet long and four feet wide, the coverings of which were luted in with lead. Each case was inscribed both in Latin and in Greek characters, one as containing the body of Numa Pompilius, son of Pompo, king of the Romans; the other as containing the books of Numa Pompilius. When they were examined by the notary, the coffin of the king was said to be empty. But the other contained two bundles of books, which were not only perfect, but also quite fresh in appearance, *recentissima specie*. Each bundle contained seven rolls. One set were in Latin, and treated of the pontifical law; the other set were in Greek, and contained a system of philosophy, which was said to be that of Pythagoras. As was customary, the city praetor had them submitted to him, and finding that they were dangerous to religion, he commanded them to be burnt. This took place before a public assembly, by the hands of the assistants at the sacrifices.[1]

During the long history of Rome, whenever the popular mind was stirred by those portents and

[1] Liv. xl. 29.

wonders which we have already examined, the sacred college were bidden to betake themselves to the Sibylline prophecies, and to declare the measures which were there indicated as needful in order that the gods might be appeased. In fact the board of fifteen was a powerful engine in repressing the superstitious ferments to which the announcement of wonders, and the utterances of popular oracles, gave rise. The rites prescribed by them generally sufficed to allay the religious scruples of the citizens. On the other hand it was illegal for a private individual to announce the will of heaven, or indeed, to be in possession of oracles at all. Three years after the battle of Cannae, the city praetor gave orders that all books of prophecy, of prayer, and of sacrifice should be brought in to him before an appointed day. This order is echoed in an injunction, which Augustus directed against the private possession of books of prophecy. Here he was true to the traditional policy of the Roman Government, by which all extraordinary procedure in religion was kept under its control.[1]

In a like spirit, Tiberius attempted to put down the oracles which abounded in the neighbourhood of Rome, but with imperfect success. The Lots of Praeneste were too deeply rooted in the reverence of the public. When the cautious Emperor yielded to this feeling, a miraculous explanation was to hand.

---

[1] Liv xxv. 1. Tac. *Ann.* vi. 12.

It was said that the lots were put in a sealed case and brought to Rome. When the case was opened they were no longer to be found, but reappeared when the box was taken back to Praeneste. In accordance with the traditions of his house, the Emperor was somewhat contemptuous in his attitude towards the current beliefs. There was a great flood at Rome in the year following upon the death of Augustus, and a proposal was made in the Senate that the Sibylline books should be consulted. Tiberius, however, refused, and sent for the water engineer, *curator aquarum*. We can understand the dislike such a character as his would inspire among the more superstitious, and might even be led to discount the slanders which befoul his name, when we recall the abuse which the Jesuits of the seventeenth century poured forth upon Scaliger. He was as little likely to obtain justice at the hands of the people, as of his political opponents, the high nobility.

The use of lots seems to have depended at first upon a magic property attributed to them. It is in some such confidence that the fetish priest in Guinea shuffles the strips of leather that make up his bundle. Although in later times the Roman saw, in the employment of the lots, an appeal to the goddess of chance, he still thought of them as possessing a lucky character in themselves. When we throw a coin into the air, in order to decide something by the way in which it falls, we see in the act nothing beyond a purely mechanical process. We have to make at least two corrections in our thought, if we wish to enter into the Roman feeling. In the first place, there is the magical property of the lot itself, as we have just seen. Further, the behaviour of the lot bears witness to some influence; perhaps to the will of some spirit.[1]

The Romans were in this respect at the same stage of culture as their northern neighbours. The Germans, say Tacitus, had a simple way of dealing with lots. They cut off a branch from a fruit-bearing tree, and divided it into pieces, each of which they marked. These were scattered at random over a cloth. If the appeal was a public one, a priest officiated; if a private one, then the head of the family. He prayed to the gods, and, looking up to heaven, picked up three of the pieces of wood in succession. These he interpreted according to the marks made upon them.[2]

The Lots of Praeneste were connected with the impressive worship of Fortuna Primigenia. She, "the eldest born," was regarded as the mother of Jupiter and of Juno, and held them as children in her arms. Questions were put to her. The answers were given by oaken lots, which a boy drew from a case made of the wood of a sacred olive tree; they were shuffled carefully before they were drawn.

[1] Tylor, *Prim. Cult.* i. 78.   [2] *Germania*, 10.

Coins are extant on which the box and the boy appear. Elsewhere such lots were made of poplar wood or of fir. The story of the repulse of Tiberius shows that they were really viewed as fetishes.[1]

In drawing lots the Romans sometimes used an urn with a narrow neck. When it was filled with water only one lot could rise to the top at a time. The number of them was carefully adjusted before the drawing took place to the number of the participants. Horace compares the call of destiny, whether it summons us to die, or to a change of fortune, with the appearance of the lot at the brim of the urn. "All we are driven to the same goal. Sooner or later the lot of each will come forth from the urn, and will set us on board ship for that exile which never ends!"[2]

The lot was employed in some of the most important transactions of government. It determined the provinces which fell to the lot of the consuls, and selected the quaestors who should preside over important trials. This mode of appealing to chance was easy to employ and interpret. We may set it first among the *artificial* modes of divination.

We now pass to omens which require special skill in drawing out their meaning.

Perhaps the most characteristic mode of divining at Rome was by observing the flight and the song of birds. Hence they were classified into the singers,

[1] Cic. *Div.* ii. 86.　　　　[2] Hor. *Odes*, II. iii. 25.

oscines, under which head came the raven, the crow, and the owl, and the flyers, *praepetes*. It was the first bird seen or heard that gave the omen. This was auspicious as a rule when the bird appeared on the left. Meaningless as all this appears now to us, and indeed to the cultured Roman of the time of Cicero, it was once viewed as the communication of spirit to spirit. As the countryman walked round his land he was greeted and warned by the winged inhabitants of the trees. But it was only to "the people of the spear" that the wood spirits so revealed the future. No plebeian, no newcomer that is, could so ascertain the will of the gods. One who was not a patrician could not take the auspices, even though he were a magistrate. "According to the custom of the elders," says Livy, "the auspices were confined to the fathers." The belief that the birds were endowed with some measure of insight was familiar to Job. In order to mark the secrecy of wisdom, he says that it is "kept close from the fowls of the air."[1]

If the Lots of Praeneste remind us of fetishes, the augurs remind us of medicine men. They seem to come from an immemorial past. Some ancient rules bear testimony to the importance of their office. Once an augur always an augur. When other priests were condemned and sent into exile, their place was filled by another; an augur, though

---

[1] *Job*, xxviii. 21.

he were found guilty of the gravest crimes, kept his office for life. Again, if he had a sore upon his body he was not allowed to take the sacred seat and watch the birds. There was a similar Levitical injunction. "No man that was scabbed might offer fire offerings." The augurs were not allowed to have coverings upon their lamps, but must leave them open always.[1]

Like many other offices in the religion of Rome, that of augur was said to have been instituted by King Numa. According to tradition there were no augurs in the reign of Romulus. At first they were three in number, one for each of the tribes. When a plebeian was chosen as dictator in 328 B.C., the augurs were consulted as to the validity of the election. They at once declared that the omens had been adverse. This did great credit to their insight. For the dictator was named at night and in silence by the consul in his camp, and he communicated with no one as to the election. The augurs, however, though they were sitting at Rome, perceived, doubtless by a sort of telepathy, what, in particular, vitiated the transaction. But all this insight went for nothing. In the year 300 B.C. the plebeians obtained entry into the sacred college itself, and five augurs were elected from among them. We can imagine the horror with which such an innovation was viewed by the more conservative Romans.[2]

The most famous name in the history of Roman

---

[1] Plut. *R. Q.* 99, 73, 72.　　[2] Liv. iv. 4; viii. 23.

augury was that of Attus Navius. From his earliest years he was marked out as a seer. As a boy, he got a meagre livelihood by tending swine. One day one of his charges were missing, and the poor swine-herd vowed to give the largest bunch of grapes in the vineyard to the god, if the pig were found again. When this happened, he might have been expected to trust his eyesight in picking out the largest bunch; but Attus was not an ordinary person. After the wandering pig was found, Attus stood in the middle of the vineyard with his look directed towards the south. He marked off the sky into four parts, and the birds warned him off three. He then divided the fourth quarter into regions, and with the help of his winged advisers, lighted upon a bunch of marvellous size. "So we find it written," says Cicero. When this feat of Attus became known he acquired great reputation, and was consulted by all the neighbourhood. His fame went on spreading until it reached King Tarquin the First, at Rome, and he was summoned to court. The king proposed to make an alteration in the constitution of the Roman cavalry, and the augur opposed this on the ground that what had once been done in obedience to augury, could not be altered or added to unless the birds were favourable. The king was angry and ridiculed the augural discipline. "Come now, oh prophet," he said, "discover by augury whether what I am thinking of, can be done." Attus obeyed and answered "Yes." The king then said, "I was thinking that a grindstone could be cut with a razor." And he commanded Attus to make the attempt. The stone was brought into the presence of the king, and before the eyes of the assembly Attus cut it in two with the razor. After this marvellous proof of his powers Attus was at once appointed court augur, and was resorted to by the people also with reference to their own private affairs. The stone and razor were buried on the very spot where all this happened. An enclosure kept off the profane from the sacred spot. The statue of Attus, with his head veiled as if exercising his art, was set up on the left of the steps of the senate-house for a memorial to those who came after, *ad posteros miraculi eius monumentum.* "So great," says Livy, "was the respect which was thenceforth paid to the priesthood of the augurs, that nothing was done by the Romans either at home or abroad without consulting the augurs, and where the birds were not favourable all transactions were invalid."[1]

In addition to public auspices private ones were taken upon all occasions of importance. At marriage ceremonies, the bird watcher, *auspex*, had to take care that nothing should be done in defiance of the birds. The presence of this official was regarded as essential, long after the practice of taking the auspices had fallen into disuse. When Marcia was married again to the

[1] Cic. *Div.* i. 31 ff. Liv. i. 36.

younger Cato, every circumstance of merriment and feasting was omitted. "They are joined in silence, content that Brutus is auspex."[1]

The spot from which the auspices were taken at Rome, *auguraculum*, was on the Capitol. Here the augur took his seat with veiled head, holding in his right hand a curved wand, or *lituus*, which was free from knots. Then he looked forth over the city and country, and after a prayer to the gods, marked off the regions of the sky from east to west. He declared the right hand to be towards the south and the left towards the north. No buildings were allowed to be erected which interfered with his outlook. The limit within which the auspices were viewed, was set by the *pomoerium*, or open space within and without the city wall. At first the birds were observed within the boundaries of the Palatine Hill. This space grew with the city, but did not include the Aventine Hill. Neither Servius Tullius, nor Sulla, nor Caesar brought it into the declared bounds of the city for augural purposes. This was left to the emperor Claudius. The leaving out of the Aventine was accounted for by a story about Romulus and Remus. The two brothers were rivals for the honour of giving a name to the new city, and agreed to leave the decision to the guardian spirits of the neighbourhood. Romulus took the Palatine Hill for the field of his augury; Remus, the Aventine. Remus was the first to have

---

[1] Lucan, ii. 371.

a good omen. He saw six vultures. Romulus, however, saw twelve. The partisans of each acclaimed their leader as king. A tumult followed, and Remus was killed. "Hence," said Messalla, "all those who have advanced the sacred bounds of the city, have excluded the Aventine as being possessed by birds of ill omen." The augural wand of Romulus, which he employed on this occasion, was preserved in the court-house of the Salii, on the Palatine. Although the building was burnt down on one occasion, the wand remained unharmed.[1]

When a general was in the field, he took the omens before the battle from the behaviour of the sacred chickens. They were kept in a cage. When the auspices were taken the attendants, *pullarii*, threw them a cake. If the fragments fell from their beaks to the ground as they pecked at their food, the omen was good. It was called *tripudium solistimum*, in the archaic language of Roman ritual. At the moment of taking the auspices, the general summoned a skilled augur to his side, and said " I wish you to help me in the auspices." " I have heard," was the reply. In order that they might be taken duly, there must be no interfering circumstances. The absence of these was called *silence*. The general proceeds : " Say whether there seems to be silence." The augur looks neither up nor around, and answers that there seems to be silence. " Say whether they will feed." " They

____
[1] Liv. i. 18, 7. Gell. *N. A.* xiii. 14   Cic. *Div.* i. 30.

feed," is the response. It was a bad omen if they were slow in coming out of their cage, or if they refused to drink. The hunger and the thirst of the chickens seem to have been interpreted as signs of their soundness.[1]

Once in a war with the Samnites, the ardour of the Roman forces was so great, that in their desire for the conflict, those who were officiating at the auspices, falsely reported favourable omens to the general. He gave the order to begin battle, but was informed in the meantime of the deceit that had been practised. " Let him who assisted at the auspices," he cried, "receive the penalty if he gives a false report. His good report is a sufficient omen to the Roman people and the army." The attendants were set by his orders in the front line of the troops, and just before the engagement began the guilty man fell, pierced by a javelin. " The gods are here in the battle," shouted the general, "and the guilty man is punished." As he uttered these words a raven croaked loudly before the consul. In his joy at this augury, he declared that the gods had never been more manifestly present with human beings.[2]

It appears from this that the augur could only report the auspices when he was called upon. The practical sense of the Romans is credited sometimes with this contrivance, by which the omens were kept from interfering unduly with public business. In

Cic. *Div.* ii. 71. Plut. *def. or.* 49.   [2] Liv. x. 40.

religion, however, we must be on our guard against applying our own conceptions of what is reasonable to ancient customs. The augur was not permitted to intrude unasked upon the magistrate, for the simple reason that the magistrate was supposed himself to take the auspices, and the augur was merely his assistant. "In the discipline of the augurs it is established," says Pliny, "that evil omens and auspices have no bearing upon those who are engaged in any undertaking, if they say that they have not taken note of them." And he sees in this a mark of the divine indulgence.

At the same time, a general who did not comply with the traditional practice, exposed himself to severe accusations if he failed in his campaigns. The disaster of Lake Trasimenus was put down in part to the neglect of the consul Flaminius, who, before setting out, had omitted to take the auspices. In the first Punic war a Roman admiral, who was delayed by the refusal of the sacred chickens to eat, ordered them to be plunged into water that they might be compelled to drink. But his impiety was followed by the defeat of his fleet.[1]

Folklore, like ancient medicine, is anything rather than squeamish. The Etruscans used to ascertain the future by inspecting the entrails of the victims used in sacrifices, and in particular, the liver, the lungs, and the heart. It was from Etruria that the

[1] Liv. xxii. i. Cic. *N. D.* ii. 7.

haruspices, the officiating priests, came originally. Hence when the Romans were at war with their northern neighbours, they were deprived of the services of the haruspices. Not to be beaten, they kidnapped a Tuscan priest, and learnt from him what they wanted. Two hundred years later they were still sending for these foreigners. Cicero, in his ideal body of law, ordains that prodigies and portents should be referred to the haruspices of Etruria at the discretion of the Senate, and that Etruria should teach the discipline to the chief magistrates.[1]

The head of the liver was most carefully examined. If it was lacking, the omen was of the worst kind. It happened to M. Marcellus just before he went to meet his death fighting against Hannibal; to Gaius Marius, when he was sacrificing at Utica; to Caligula, on the first day of the year in which he was assassinated; and to his successor, Claudius, in the month before he was carried off by poison.[2] If the lung was indented, the priest put off the business about which he was consulted. The heart of the victim was not inspected until the time when Pyrrhus left Italy, L. Postumius Albinus being the king of worship. On the day when the Dictator Caesar began to wear the purple and to employ a chair of gold, he was sacrificing, and found no heart in the

---

[1] Liv. v. 17; xxvii. 37. Cic. *Legg.* ii. 21.
[2] Plin. *N. H.* xi. 189. Liv. viii. 9.

ox. The omen was undoubted. There was great dispute, however, among the more learned, whether the victim could have lived without this important organ, or whether it lost it at the time of the sacrifice. On the other hand, when Augustus was sacrificing at Spoleto, on his first day of office, the livers of six victims were found to have double folds, and it was prophesied therefrom that he should double his empire within the year. In Brandenburg this kind of omen is still believed in. "When a pig is killed, and the spleen is found to be turned over, there will be another overthrow, namely, a death in the family within the year." This mode of divination, at first used at Rome under exceptional circumstances, gained its place alongside the more ancient forms of divination by lot and by the observation of birds. It passed into private use, and the viscera of frogs and dogs were consulted by the curious.[1]

Thunder would seem to have been viewed as ominous from very early times. It was to Etruria, however, that the Romans owed their more developed system of divination by this means. While other omens were not thought to interfere with the holding of the burgess meetings, an ancient commentary said, "If Jove thunders or lightens, it is wrong to hold them." For other purposes lightning, provided it came from the left, was of the best omen. Before

[1] Cic. *Div.* i. 85. Plin. *N. H.* xi. 186. Tylor, *Prim. Cult.* i. 124.

the comitia were held, a tent was pitched outside the city in order to observe the auspices. The tent was not thought to be pitched properly, unless the magistrate took the auspices before crossing the pomoerium. When Antony adjourned the elections on the ground of an adverse omen, he did so as augur. Cicero reproached him with not knowing that the augur had merely the right of giving a report, and that, as consul, he himself had the right of observing the heavens.[1]

The Etruscans reduced their lightning lore to an elaborate system. Their scriptures taught that nine gods sent the lightning, and that it was of eleven kinds, of which Jove sent three. The Romans knew two only of these deities. They put down to Jove lightning that came in the day, and night lightning to Summanus. Etruria thought further that some kinds of lightning came from the earth ; those which they called nether, *infera*, were especially terrible and accursed. Much weight was attributed to those omens by lightning which presented themselves to a man on founding his household.[2]

Roughly speaking, the interest of the Romans in astrology was confined at first to the themes of Iopas, the bard of Carthage, who sang of the wanderings of the moon and the sun's eclipse. Each month began with the new moon, and the midway

---

[1] Cic. *Div.* i. 33 ; ii. 42. *Phil.* ii. 81.
[2] Plin. *N. H.* ii. 138.

division answered to the full moon. Before the secretary of Appius Claudius published the order of the year, the junior pontiff had the duty of watching for the new moon, and of reporting her appearance immediately to the king of worship. On the night of the 3rd of September, 168 B.C., when the Roman forces were in Macedonia, there was an eclipse of the moon. This occurrence, which otherwise would have been regarded as a terrible portent by the soldiers, was viewed with less alarm, since a military tribune, C. Sulpicius Gallus, assembled the troops the night before with the permission of the consul, and gave a lecture on the approaching eclipse of the moon, in which he showed how it was caused by the earth's shadow. The lecturer obtained a brilliant reputation when everything turned out as he had prophesied. The spread of astronomical science was very slow, however. A century and a half later, it was remembered with awe that the orb of the sun was pale during the year in which Caesar was assassinated, and in the time of the war with Antony.[1]

Systematic astrology obtained a footing in Italy, as soon as Rome came into close contact with the East. Cato enjoined upon his ideal farm bailiff that he was not to consult a Chaldaean. The professors of the art came soon so prominently into notice that the praetor peregrinus, in 139 B.C., ordered them to

[1] Liv. xliv. 37. Plin. *N. H.* ii. 98.

get clear of Italy within ten days. But law and order were no more successful than they ever are when they come into conflict with superstition. Fortunes continued to be told, horoscopes to be cast, predictions to be made. Although no reason was given for them, or perhaps could be given, the Romans were glad to learn such important facts as these, that the conjunction of Jupiter or Venus with the Moon was beneficial at the birth of a child, while her conjunction with Mars or Saturn was adverse. A friend of Cicero, Lucius Tarutius Firmanus, who was an expert astrologer, cast the horoscope of the city, and ascertained that it was indeed founded on the feast of the Parilia. This harmony of science and tradition must have been welcomed, especially when it was confirmed by detailed facts. Firmanus assigned to the moon her exact position. She was in the constellation of Libra at the time. He was thus enabled to go on to predict the destiny of the city. This triumph of astrology in fields where by the nature of the case verification was impossible, is somewhat overclouded, when Cicero goes on to tell us that contemporary astrologers foretold to Crassus, Pompey, and Caesar, that they should die in old age, at home, and in full possession of their reputation. All three died violent deaths. Such, alas, is the fate of prophecies which condescend to particulars! Tarutius also supplied a number of most precise and interesting details concerning the birth, the life, and the death, of that entirely imaginary person Romulus. This was at the request of the great savant Varro.[1]

Horace was fond of listening to the astrologers who practiced their art in the purlieus of the Great Circus. He did not know, however, what his own horoscope was. This strikes one as rather a mean trait in the character of that genial man of the world. He used often to get an afternoon's amusement in this way, and yet never put his hand in his pocket and patronised the adepts. Possibly, however, he was alarmed. He strongly advises a lady friend not to make any use of the astrological tables of the Chaldaeans. He requests her particularly not to find out the term of life appointed for him. Perhaps we can appreciate this scruple of Horace when we learn how such prophecies had an unpleasant way of getting themselves realised punctually, or even accelerated by officious acquaintances. Tables of the kind to which Horace refers, were employed by an adept whose acquaintance I had the pleasure of making a short time since.[2]

As the astrologers rose in influence and favour, they received generally the more dignified name of mathematicians, *mathematici*, which the populace had already bestowed upon them. Even the grave historian Tacitus himself seems to attach a certain

---

[1] Cic. *Div.* i. 85. Plut. *Rom.* 12.
[2] Hor. *Carm.* i. 11 ; ii. 17. *Serm.* i. 6, 114.

weight to their predictions, although he is not blind to the evils they cause. He speaks of them as a class of men who are faithless to the powerful, and deceive those who trust in them. Yet he foresees that however often they be forbidden to practice their art, they will always find dupes. Two years after the death of Augustus, they were banished by the order of the Senate. But the patronage of the Emperors themselves was extended to them, so that such regulations remained a dead letter. Tiberius, who believed in nothing else except thunderstorms, placed unbounded faith in the Chaldaeans. He had studied the art under Thrasyllus, whom he put to a severe test.[1]

As often as Tiberius consulted an astrologer, he used to take him to a remote part of his palace. One attendant alone used to be present, chosen for his ignorance and bodily strength. After the interview the adept was conducted away along a precipitous path. The palace overhung the cliffs, and if the noble owner entertained a suspicion that the man was an impostor, or was acting in bad faith, he was thrown over into the sea. In this way the danger of disclosure of any secrets was prevented. Thrasyllus was led along the same road, and was asked whether he had cast his own horoscope. He took some observations, and displayed the greatest alarm, and at last said that he was in the utmost

____
[1] Tac. *Hist.* i. 22 ; *Ann.* vi. 21.

peril. Tiberius thereupon embraced him, and congratulated him upon his admirable foresight. Ever afterwards he treated what Thrasyllus said as the answers of an oracle. The knowledge of the art passed on to Thrasyllus' son, who prophesied the accession of Nero.

Tiberius himself reached a high pitch of proficiency. He foretold that Galba would one day reign, and in his last hours revealed the career of his successor Gaius. Otho, in like manner, surrounded himself with seers and Chaldaeans. These promised to him that he should outlive Nero and rule over the Romans. Two generations later the philosopher Favorinus wrote a tractate against all this, in which he set forth the arguments which were as sound then as now—and as little regarded. Tacitus himself must be credited with very respectable prophetic powers. Two thousand years nearly have passed since he wrote, and the Chaldaeans are still with us.[1]

[1] Tac. *Ann.* vi. 20. Plut. *Galb.* 23.

THE PRIMITIVE IDEA OF HOLINESS

WE have seen how very flexible are the primitive ideas of cause and effect. But these ideas are not applied to the whole of Nature with the disinterestedness of the man of science. The savage is as impatient as Lord Macaulay was, with every train of thought that does not end in some practical utility. And he soon singles out from his surroundings those things that seem to stand in some special relation to himself, his belongings, and his interests. For him all explanation must take a concrete form. "You cannot explain things to the Oriental," says Mr. Kipling, "you must show." And here the Oriental is like his primitive brother. Romer once peeped in at an open door, and found an old negro caboceer sitting amid twenty thousand fetishes in his private fetish museum, thus performing his devotions. The old man told him that he did not know the hundredth part of the use they had been to him. His ancestors and he had collected them. Each one had done some service. The visitor took up a stone about as big as a hen's egg, and the owner told its history. He was once going out on important business, but crossing the threshold he trod on this stone and hurt himself. "Ha ha!" thought he, "Are you here?" So he took up the stone, and it helped him in his undertaking for days.[1]

This kind of association may attach itself to all manner of things, to minerals, plants, human beings, and places. But the benefit which is thus promised can also be ensured by parts of these objects. A lump of soil from a lucky spot, a feather from a bird, a few threads from the garment of a luck-bringing individual, are sufficient by the rules of savage logic. The influence of the fetish is interpreted as a kind of life of which the fetish is the seat. It is needless to go far afield for analogies. The belief in charms is widely prevalent still, and is of the same kind exactly as the belief in fetishes. The protection employed against lightning, the onions, the hair, the sprats' heads, of which Roman folklore gives so amusing an explanation, is obviously of the same kind with the fetishes of the African. Roman medicine furnishes us with many talismans which, strange apparently, would be proper enough in the eyes of a savage. The feeling that you, dear reader, have some things that bring luck, brings even you in touch with the poor heathen who collects such things into his fetish museum, and does reverence to them.

Over against lucky things stand those which are

---

[1] Tylor, *Prim. Cult.* ii. 158.

unlucky.   Just as the belief in charms is echoed very faintly in your and my belief in lucky things, so in the shrinking we have towards what seems unlucky, we catch a very faint whisper of the thunderous threatenings which baneful objects and actions seem to hold out against the savage.   Native Australians in sound health have been known to die of terror within twenty-four hours, after they have been placed under some taboo.   There is no reason, therefore, to doubt the stories current among the Romans of the death of persons who in like manner have come under a taboo.   The man who named the secret name of the city may indeed have died.   The families of the Potitii may indeed have wasted away, as Livy describes ; if, when they divulged their family worship of Hercules, they broke any very binding taboo.   And it is not impossible that the death of Atticus' grandmother may have been accelerated by her anxiety about the proper carrying out of the Alban festival.

The number of things and actions that were tabooed at Rome in historical times, was always tending to grow less.   What once was a general prohibition, is limited to special occasions in the life of the individual or to the priests.   The Flamen of Jupiter was always on his guard against breaking a very elaborate series of taboos.   There is reason to suppose that in prehistoric times, the lifetime of the ordinary citizen was cumbered much in the same way.

We can distinguish two applications of these pro-
hibitions. On the one hand it was desired to protect
the life of the priest or citizen against harm, and he
was warned off from given objects or the performance of given actions. On the other hand, human
beings might be regarded as sources of danger, and
they became tabooed in the same way as the leaven,
the raw flesh, dogs, and goats were tabooed to the
Flamen. Such for example was the outlaw, the man
who by some act had become a source of harm to
the community. In order that he might not transmit
any evil to the sacred elements, fire and water, he was
carefully prevented from using them. Lest the blood
of the criminal should be shed and the land become
polluted, he was either driven into exile by the
operation of this taboo, whereby the necessity of his
death was done away; or, if it were necessary, he was
made to leap from the Tarpeian rock. It was thence
that the tribunes cast Manlius down. So, too, a
tribune to gratify private spite, seized a Metellus
who had been censor, and would have hurled him
down the same precipice, unless another tribune
had interposed his veto. The Arabs who killed
Professor Palmer, made him leap from a precipice,
thus, as they thought, avoiding bloodguiltiness. We
are reminded of the care with which the Romans
avoided a like stain, when they buried the sinning
vestal alive in the Accursed Field.[1]

[1] Liv. vi. 20. Plin. *N. H.* vii. 143.

Although the greatest care might be exercised, it was impossible but that from time to time evil influences should be encountered unawares. Death seems to have been viewed as one of the most important causes of taboo. The Flamen of Jupiter might not touch a corpse, or indeed, step upon a grave. The white garments and headbands worn by women who were in mourning, were the outward marks of the temporary taboo in which they found themselves. At Argos the white garments worn in mourning were specially washed in water, as if for purification. At Rome the cypress which stood at the entrance to the house of death, warned those who were about to engage in religious ceremonies that they were not to enter.[1]

If we wish to understand the primitive view of impurity, we must extend the notion to all the cases in which a man breaks one of the traditional taboos.

Let us suppose that such has been the case; that either voluntarily, as in the example of the mourner, or involuntarily, someone has broken a taboo. There were means to restore him. At Rome, both fire and water were believed to have this power. The bystanders at a funeral removed all pollution which they had incurred, by sprinkling themselves with water; sometimes they stepped over fire. When Aeneas joined his father by the temple of Ceres in the fields, he avoided touching the sacred vessels

and the images of the gods. " Take them, O father,"
he said, " I may not handle them until I have washed
my stains away in living water." Special virtues
were thus attributed to running water. It was alive,
or else how should it move? This belief influenced
the baptismal procedure of the early Church. Since
the hands were very likely to have become impure,
" all commencement of worship," said a young
Roman, "warns away those who have not pure
hands." " There are partial washings or purifications," says Lane, "which all Muslims perform on
certain occasions, even if they neglect their prayers,
and which are considered as religious acts." [1]

Since water has such magic powers, a bath is not
to be undertaken lightly. A newborn child among
the Damaras is washed—the only time he is washed
in his life—then dried and greased, and the ceremony
is over. So the Roman ladies originally washed
their heads only once a year.[2]

At first the water is believed to remove some
natural state of the person using it, in the same
way as it removes the grime from his skin. It has
this physical office before it is brought into connection with the worship of any spirit. And it is
only as the belief in spiritual powers is sublimed and
refined, that the purification is regarded as symbolic,

[1] Festus, s v. *aqua.* Virg. *Aen.* ii. 717. *Didache*, 7. Liv. xlv. 5.
Lane, *Mod. Egypt.* c. iii.
[2] Galton, *Travels*, c. 6. Plut. *R. Q.* 100.

or rather productive, of moral purity. Every orthodox Hindu is perfectly persuaded that the dirtiest water, if taken from a sacred stream and applied to his body, either internally or externally, will purify his soul. Imperfect as such a conception seems to us, it represents an advance, nevertheless, on the primitive one. There is no doubt that the water of a running stream was believed by the Roman to take away the awful guilt of murder, to use Ovid's striking words. But these easy minds passed away, and Cicero anticipates the feelings of a later time when he says, " In truth there is no atonement for crimes against mankind, and for impiety towards the gods. Men pay the penalty of their guilt, not so much through the ministers of justice, as that they are hunted and driven by the furies, who use the anguish of conscience and the torturing sense of evil, instead of the flaming pinebrands of which the poets speak. The darts of the gods are directed against the minds of the wicked." The Roman poets did far less than those of Greece towards transforming the idea of physical pollution into that of moral guilt. This task was performed rather by philosophical writers, such as Cicero. Since, however, the public of such writers was a very small one, we are driven to the conclusion that the Romans must have been more backward in this respect than the Greeks, whose poetry could speak to all.[1]

---

[1] M. Williams, *Hinduism*, 157.   Ovid, *Fasti*, ii. 45.   Cic. *Legg.* i. 40.   *Har. Resp.* 39.   Butcher, *Greek Genius*, 128.

Fire was used in the same way as water. "The wise priest whirls round the limbs that are to be purified, a lustral torch, the flame of which is blended of dark blue sulphur and black pitch." So disease is warded off by leaping through the flames at the festival of Pales; disease being one of the most recognisable states of taboo. When the evils for which water and fire are safeguards, are referred to evil spirits, the lustral elements are thought to drive away the spirits of evil, of disease, rather than the disease itself. Hence fire gains the repute of being a charm against evil spirits, apart from their particular malign influences. "Fire," says Giraldus Cambrensis, "is the greatest of enemies to every kind of phantom, insomuch that those who have seen apparitions, fall into a swoon as soon as they are sensible of the brightness of fire." But this is contradicted by experience. I have been at spiritualist meetings, when the clairvoyant has seen many spirits, although the gas was turned up. Fire was also a charm against strangers, who on the primitive view, if not evil spirits, were at any rate in league with them. The Chinese phrase, *foreign devils*, defines itself. When the Damaras, the bushmen, the oxen, and the zebras, came out of the tree of life, the Damaras lit a fire which scared away the bushmen and the zebras, so that they themselves and the oxen were left. The taper that was kept burning in the chamber of the new-born babe at Rome, was a precaution against malign influence of all kinds.[1]

Fire and water, then, are two of the chief means by which taboo is removed. Their influence, however, on the whole seems to have been thought of as negative in character. They did not communicate strength to those who employed them. They simply removed an evil state. Other agents were needed, which should do more than this.

The desired end was the obtaining of fuller and richer life. This was needed not only for the individual, but also for his surroundings. The notion that the earth is wearing out and needs constant renewal, was forced upon the Romans by his system of farming. The rotation of crops and the use of manures was understood by him only to a small extent, and from year to year he was compelled to let his land rest. As Time passed by, he took away each hour somewhat of the strength of the land, the people, their herds, and their crops.

"The age is enfeebled," laments Lucretius, "and the earth, exhausted by bearing, scarce produces little living creatures, she who produced all races, and gave birth to the huge bodies of wild beasts. Aforetime, too, she of herself made fair harvests and lush vineyards to grow for the use of man. Sweet fruit and lush meadows gave she, which now scarce come to the full, with our toil to boot. We

<hr>

[1] Claudian, *VI. Cons. Hon.* 324. Galton, *op. cit.* c. 6. Lucr. ii. fin.

wear away our oxen and the strength of the yeomen, and though our iron wastes away, the corn fields yield but a scanty harvest. So niggardly are they of their fruit, and after so much toil do they let it grow. The sorrowful planter, too, of the worn-out and withered vine, upbraids the march of time and wearies heaven, and comprehends not that all things are wasting away piecemeal, and going to the grave forespent in the long tale of years." Antique rites promised to the worshipper renewed life for himself, his crops, and his cattle, and so to stay the continual waning of his, and their, life. The chief means by which this was attained lay in the flesh and blood of certain animals and certain men, or in the life of certain trees and herbs. Contact with the skin of the goat which the Luperci sacrificed, made the Roman women fruitful. So the blood of the October horse communicated its virtues to the flocks and the people at the Parilia. It renewed their life.

Let us now ask ourselves, on the principles of primitive thought, what consequences follow from the use of blood in worship. We might be tempted to reply at once that it will be identified with the life of the community, and point to the belief of the early Jews. It cannot be maintained, however, that there are adequate evidences of such a belief at Rome. Perhaps it is going too far to speak of it even as the vehicle of the communal life, at any rate in any unique sense.[1] There is no obvious reason why we should attribute to the use of blood in ritual a meaning different in kind from that of the use of fat. Bearing this in mind, we may take it that the application of the blood and flesh of the slaughtered animal in lustration, bound together in some way those who were present at the rite. The communal feeling, if it was not created, was at any rate nourished, by such acts.

It is a commonplace that the notion of individual existence is of comparatively recent growth, and that in nearly all ancient peoples, the life of the citizen was not conceived in separation from that of the community. This merely states in clear terms a sentiment felt deeply always, even when most obscurely expressed, namely, that each man is dependent upon his fellows ; a dependence far more strongly marked when law gave but an intermittent sanction to individual rights, than at present, when the very strength of the social sanctions causes them to be overlooked. Instead, therefore, of treating the ancient community as made up of individuals, we ought to proceed as if the community came first, and then sundered itself into the life of the separate citizens. We might, without excessive paradox, affirm that the individual only begins to exist in any speculative sense, at a comparatively recent date. When we bear in mind, on the one hand, that savage

---

[1] *Deut.* xii. 23.

life is hedged in with many more conventions than civilised ; and, on the other, that savage thought moves along fewer and narrower channels, it becomes conceivable that primitive existence is in the main a social affair. There is no loophole for private initiative, and what is more, there is comparatively little impulse towards it.

In the light of these considerations, we may go on to affirm that the communal life was that to which all considerations of utility or harm were referred, and also that all acts from which benefit was expected were of necessity communal acts.

In the first place, then, the distinctions of lucky and unlucky are drawn by preference with a view to the communal life. That which is good is good for the communal life, that which is bad at all is bad for it. Our Anglo-Saxon forefathers have left a curious testimony to this in their word "holy," or wholesome. What is wholesome is so for the whole people. And what is wholesome for the whole people gathers round it that awe which the term holy arouses in our minds. Thus what is trifling in its result for good or for ill, gains importance on this ancient view. The primitive idea of holiness then implies, as its chief element, *relation to the communal life.*

We have found reason from time to time to hold that in the main the religion of Rome was very primitive in form. Its acts of worship have rarely lost the appearance of magic; its objects of reverence are, in the main, fetishes. The abstractions with which the Roman has been credited, the spirits whose names appear in the *indigitamenta*, are really little more than the magical names by which certain actions are forwarded. This is shown by the inability of the Romans to give any further account of these spirits. It is probable that they had no existence in the Roman fancy beyond the magic of their names. Where the Roman religion rises above fetishism, it does not go beyond the lower stages of animism.[1]

Hence those who connect the notion of holiness with belief in spirits, bring the origin of this idea too far forward. At any rate the Roman idea of holiness seems to have been far more vivid than can be accounted for by their undeveloped animism. On the other hand, it is quite reasonable to suppose that the idea of holiness, which was based on the communal life, changed in content when the religious imagination rose to a genuine belief in spirits. We must consider, therefore, that Robertson Smith was dealing with a later stage of the development of the idea when he said that the term " Holy expresses the relation of natural things to the gods."[2] In other words, the more complex idea rises out of the simpler ones of fetishism and taboo, when they are brought into relation with belief in divine beings whose existence is manifested in the holy objects.

[1] p. 105.   [2] *Rel. Sem.* 90.

The spear and the flint, which once were fetishes perhaps like the stone of the caboceer, are said afterwards to be sacred to the spear god and the sky spirit, and their efficacy is referred not to any intrinsic properties, but to the influence of the deity to whom they are sacred.

It is worth notice that the strength of the communal feeling is quite adequate to account for an idea of holiness of considerable impressiveness. The *religio*, or sense of scruple, of which Roman writers speak, has not that immediate connection with the belief in spirits which the term religion suggests to us; and yet we know that it was a very powerful motive in the Roman mind. Instead of treating the reference to spirits as its primary meaning, it would seem more appropriate to treat this reference as a later development, growing out of the simpler meaning of communal duty.

There are some important indications that the social origin of the idea of holiness was always, more or less, present to the Romans. The pontiffs held that no temple or statue could be duly consecrated without the express appointment of the Roman people. This held at least of all consecrations which took place on lands belonging to the state. On the other hand, all objects that were sacred in degree lost that character when they fell into the hands of the enemy, and resumed it by a kind of *postliminium*, when they were recovered. (A Roman who was captured in war thereby lost his civil rights; he recovered them under ordinary circumstances on his return to captivity. The name *postliminium* was given to this restoration.[1])

It would appear, then, that the main element in early religious belief is the same with what is not the least important element in later forms. Relation to the Church answers very closely to the antique idea of relation to the community. The persistence with which mediaeval ecclesiastics treated all objects as sacred which belonged to the Church, helps us to understand how all objects and actions which were connected with the communal interest, gained a similar character when the State was practically identical with the religious community. If we pass to a higher level, the correspondence is still the same. "Only through society is anyone enabled to give that effect to the idea of himself as the object of his actions, to the idea of a possible better state of himself, without which the idea would remain like that of space to a man who had not the senses either of sight or of touch." And what is said here of the personality as a whole, applies especially to its religious development.[2]

Further, it is this fundamental element in the idea of holiness which enables us to understand the great

---

[1] Liv. ix. 46. Cic. *de Domo.* 136. *Dig.* xi. 7, 36. Ortolan, *Leg. Rom.* ii. 254.

[2] Green, *Prol. Eth.* p. 190.

paradox of the Greek and Roman religions. The immorality attributed to the Greek deities, and the unsympathetic — nay, lifeless — character of the Roman ones, did not touch the feeling of social duty. Here was the spring, of which the abundant waters almost swept away the mire which later tributaries poured into its stream. And so, right through the long history of both Greece and Rome, it is conceivable that the more religious natures found an outlet, imperfect indeed, for their higher feelings in the rites of what seem to us primitive or even degraded worships.

Up to this point the exact meaning that is to be attached to "holiness" in the Roman view has been indicated very vaguely. All that we have determined is that it denotes some relation to the welfare of the community, and then, by a later development, to the life of some divinity. As a matter of fact, the notion of holiness takes at least three quite distinct forms in its application to things. (We shall consider the case of persons in a future chapter.) In the first place, to follow the classification of the Roman lawyers, sacred things are those which are consecrated to the gods above, *res sacrae*. "But that land only is considered sacred which has been consecrated by the authority of the Roman people, by the passing of a law, or of a decree of the Senate. On the other hand," says Gaius, "we can, of our own free will, make land *religious* by conveying a corpse into a place which is our own property, providing only that the burial of the corpse devolves on us." The term "religious" seems to answer to a more primitive mode of thought; the presence of the dead gives rise to a species of taboo. In Cleveland, Durham, it is still believed that if a corpse is carried across a field, a public right of way is created. The notion of *sanctity* is attached to the chief possessions of the city, its walls, gates, ramparts, and senate-house. The taboo which attached to the walls of Rome is explained in the story of the death of Remus. He was said to have leapt over the line by which the walls of the city were marked out at its foundation, and to have been killed for the sacrilege which this act involved.[1]

It is striking to find that the word "pure" is employed to mark off those objects which do not come under any of these three descriptions. "That place is called pure," says Ulpian, "which is neither sacred, nor religious, nor hallowed." Hence holy things in their several kinds are marked off from amid a general assemblage of what is pure. It is not difficult to enter into the state of mind which views its surroundings in this light. According to the ancient conception, the normal state of the whole community and of its possessions was one of purity. By the careful performance of the ceremonies of its religion, two practical ends were attained. On the

---

[1] Gaius, ii. 2 ff.

one hand, water and fire put away all that was hostile to the communal life. On the other hand, the communal life was furthered and enriched by certain acts, in which the use of blood plays an important part.[1]

The fears of the State were directed to the possible interruptions of this normal condition. It will appear that those things which have been enumerated as holy in their several orders, are precisely the sources from which such dangers might be expected to come. To touch the walls by which the citizens were guarded, to disturb the spirits of the dead, to draw down the anger of the gods by trespassing on their property; such acts as these were prohibited by just that feeling of scruple which the Romans called *religio*. The aim of the Roman was not so much to ensure the activity of his gods, as to leave their peace, " the peace of the gods," unbroken ; or when it was broken, to restore it. When the reference of the changing fortunes of the State to the divine activity became more clear, both good and ill seemed to be due to the gods. The Romans at first venerated the spirits rather for their power than their goodness. They did not refuse adoration to an influential deity, although his or her moral character was unattractive. They had not reached the stage at which spirits are venerated as being higher and nobler than their worshippers. As we have seen, the ancient altar

---

[1] *Dig.* xi. 7, 2.

of Fever on the Palatine Hill, and the altar of Bad Luck on the Esquiline Hill are instances of reverence paid to evil spirits. To these may be added the mildew spirit, Robigo, whose worship was celebrated by the priest of Quirinus. Obviously, then, since the notion of deity carried with it first and chiefly the idea of power, the feeling towards the possessions and acts of the gods was one of dread. When the sacred gold was recovered from the Gauls, it was buried under the seat of Jove, in order that evil might not come through it.[1] In this way even beneficent talismans, which have been taken under the protection of a god, are avoided in the same way as other things which bring misfortune and death. Things that are holy are shunned in the same way as things that are impure. " Leaves, flowers, fruit, and water become unfit to be consumed after being consecrated to Siva."[2] Hence the term sacred meant both holy and accursed. So the same Hebrew word meant both to curse and to bless.

Nevertheless the Roman idea of holiness seems scarcely to have risen to the height which corresponding ideas attained elsewhere. The national deities were so obscurely figured, that they never entered into so living a union with their peoples as the more clearly limned gods of Greece, or the Baalim of the Semites. All the feeling of the Roman spent itself upon the worship of his ancestors, the

[1] Cic. *Legg.* ii. 28.   [2] M. Williams, *Hinduism*, 100.

elders, "the good people" among whom he lived. Hence when we pass from the notions of fetish and taboo to the same notions as transformed by contact with more developed worship, the change is less than the answering transition among the Greeks and the Hebrews. Where another would justify an act by its relation to a god, the Roman was still satisfied if he could point to the custom of the elders.

HOLY PLACES AND IDOLATRY

WHEN the primitive man begins to attribute the magical properties of objects to indwelling spirits, he finds scope for this tendency in the fire on his hearth, in the spring, the living stream, the woodland, and the mountain. The good which seems to come from water, fire, trees, and herbs, is now referred to fountain and river spirits, fire spirits, and tree spirits. If he is imaginative these creations of his fancy become free of their material embodiment, and lead lives of more or less varied character. The Roman seems to have been able just to give these ideal beings life; and there he rested. His spirits do little else than attend to the function for which, according to the pontiffs, they are told off. When, however, a spirit is attached to some fixed and familiar spot, the tangible character of his abode supplies the least imaginative worshipper with the needed suggestion. Here there is just that concrete element from which, by the usual association, the whole notion of the spirit gains life and intensity. Hence the sanctity of particular places plays an important part in the development of Roman mythology.

"The nature of the god," says Robertson Smith, "did not determine the place of his sanctuary, but the features of his sanctuary had an important share in determining the development of ideas as to the functions of the god."[1] And among the features of the sanctuary we must include the customs already bound up with it. The worship of Fortune at Praeneste was built up of many diverse elements, in which Jupiter, Juno, and divination by lots, are found. At Rome, also, the many places on the Capitoline Hill, to which sanctity was attached, determined the worship of the deities upon it. The temple of Jove was also that of Juno, Minerva, and Terminus. The peculiar form which the religious imagination took in the mind of the Romans, their scrupulous adherence to ancient names, and the faintness with which they pictured their deities, reconciled them to shrines in which many worships were carried on side by side. Among peoples of a warmer fancy they would all have been fused into the leading worship, the minor ones losing separate existence. Where, however, religious rites were practised for their magical efficacy, and were not explicitly attached to any given deity, there was less difficulty in blending them into the ritual of the adjoining temple.

[1] *Rel. Sem.* 129.

At first the sacred spot was not marked by any building. Many facts lead to the conclusion that the Romans celebrated public worship in the open air, and were without covered temples, until a very late date. That part of the great Capitoline temple which was sacred to Terminus was open to the sky, and the reason given by Servius is that sacrifice was made to him in the open air. This usage is explained in turn when we bear in mind the great antiquity of the worship of Terminus. There were other traces of this early open-air worship. It was customary for the Roman boys to go out of doors when they were about to swear by Hercules. "The temples of Dius Fidius had a hole made specially in the roof under which one might swear." In this way, too, we can understand the glorious opening by which the Pantheon is lit. Standing in the middle of the great domed chamber, one is also immediately under the dome of the sky.[1]

When any place had been marked out by a striking occurrence as holy, that is, as the seat of magical influences, or at a later time as favoured by some spirit, it was enclosed. Hence the enclosure which marked the resting place of the razor and whetstone of Attus Navius. So at Praeneste, the place to which Numerius Suffustius was directed in a dream, and where the lots were found, was guarded in like manner. The end gained by such enclosure was

---

[1] Plut. *R. Q.* 28. Jevons, pref. *R. Q.* 52.

twofold. On the one hand the citizen was protected from treading unwittingly upon enchanted ground, thereby exposing himself to unknown dangers. On the other hand the community was saved from the anger which such profanation might inspire in the national deities. This latter notion swallowed up the older one, and the belief that the god owned sacred places, seemed to explain the other form of scruple as well. There was less need to enclose the sacred spring or wood or stream, because their sacred character was manifest to all. The shepherd who sat under a holy tree or traversed a sacred wood, or plucked its leaves for his sheep, was recognised to have trespassed on the guardian spirit. The Field Brethren had a special ceremony by which they atoned for cutting down the laurels in their wood by the Tiber. In Sweden certain trees that stand free, like *that single elm tree bright against the west*, are not allowed to be hewn down, since the spirit that dwells in the tree is unwilling. But this reference to the displeasure of a spirit is obviously of later growth than the belief that the tree was the seat of direct influence upon the lives of the people who lived in its neighbourhood. The idolatrous Israelites sacrificed "under oaks and poplars and terebinths, because the shadow thereof was good."[1]

In the notion of asylum we have an interesting

---

[1] Cic. *Div.* ii. 85. Ovid, *Fasti*, iv. 749. Wilm. *Inss.* 2883. Mannhardt, *A. F. W.* i. 39. *Hosea*, iv. 13

testimony to the power of certain places to transmit their virtues to him who enters upon them. There was such a spot in the hollow between the two summits of the Capitoline Hill. But the wall by which it was marked out, was raised to such a height by the cautious Romans, that the refugee found it impossible to enter and so gain its protection. A legend was current which explained the sanctity of the place. When the city was being founded, Romulus desired to increase the number of the inhabitants at any cost. Hence he enticed to Rome all those who had been guilty of any offence, by offering them this place as an asylum. The most ancient temples were also thought to give a sacro-sanct character to those who took refuge in them. But this privilege was not extended to the temples of divinities introduced at a later time; as though the right of asylum attached to the oldest sacred places in Rome, and not to others. This dignity was conferred upon the temple which the young Octavian built in honour of Caesar, alone among later foundations. Sometimes the sacred spot was to be avoided. It could do harm to those who came upon it unlicensed. The shepherd felt compunction if he took his flock to shelter from the hailstorm in one of those temples which were scattered over the country side.[1]

We have seen that a distinction may be drawn

___

[1] Dio C. xlvii. 19. Ovid, *Fasti*, iv. 756.

between the wood spirits, the fauns, and the like on the one hand ; and the gods on the other. The gods have individuality, the other spirits have not. It seems more than likely that this individualising of the god is largely due to the association of his worship with a single place. We can trace this process even in the case of Silvanus. It is very probable that, in like manner, the worship of Juno, as a single deity, arose from a belief in a class of spirits. So long as sacred rites are celebrated chiefly by detached families or groups of families, the objects of their worship are regarded as separate. When, however, they unite to resort to some single holy place or temple, the idea that the object of their worship is also one, begins to press in upon them. "The founding of the Capitoline temple," says the author of *Ecce Homo*, "may have modified Roman religion considerably. It probably answers in Roman history to the foundation of Solomon's temple in Jewish." Yet even before the great temple was built, the god was believed to reveal himself in the crashes of thunder that were heard from the sacred hill. The untutored Roman could see him passing to and fro with his dark shield, and gathering the clouds. For it was believed that the deity was again to be found in those places where he had once appeared to his worshippers. This held good of others as well as Jupiter. After an earthquake, Juno spoke from her temple and informed her worshippers what sacrifices were necessary. Thus the place where a god has once manifested himself, becomes holy. As a matter of fact such appearances are generally recorded of places previously marked out as of magical influence. The worship of Jupiter and Juno was carried on where there were already sacred stones or sacred lots. "The physical characters that mark out a holy place," says Robertson Smith, "are not to be explained by conjectures based on the more developed types of heathenism, but must be regarded as taken over from the primitive beliefs of savage man."[1]

What is the cause, then, that gives rise to the higher conception of deity, as opposed to that of "spirit" worship? The answer is already implied. When the community gathers together for a common worship, the object of that worship transfers to itself, to a greater or less extent, the characters of the surrounding social life. "The Roman world of gods was a higher counterpart, an ideal reflection of the earthly Rome." Conversely the nobility of the national gods is a measure of the nobility of the national life. Where religion is stereotyped into a mere tradition, it acts as a check upon spiritual advance, so far as it acts at all. It is fortunate, too, that when religion does become stereotyped, its influence ceases. Nowhere is this more true than in ancient Rome.[2]

[1] Seeley, pref. Liv. i. p. 95. R. Smith, *Rel. Sem.* 130.
[2] Mommsen, *R. H. I.* 171 (Trans.)

From the notion of a holy place, and perhaps we may add, from the respect paid to the stones which so often marked such places, there sprang certain ideas about altars and images which we will now consider.   There survived to quite a late date, in the worship of Terminus, what appears to be a kind of fetichism.   Round each farm, as round each house, there was a strip of land, several feet wide, which divided it from the adjoining domains.   This was regarded as sacred and left untilled.   Stones and trunks of trees were set up at intervals along this space, which, says Dionysius, the Romans treated as gods.   At them they offered cakes and other first-fruits.   If a man moved one of these termini he might be killed as an outlaw.   Among the Israelites, also, outlawry was the penalty for the man that removed his neighbour's landmark.   From time to time during the year the master of the Roman farm went round his land singing ancient hymns, and offering sacrifice at the termini, which were wreathed with flowers for the occasion.[1]

In the stones reverenced by primitive peoples it is probable that we find the origin of the *altar* and the image.   When sacrifice was made, the blood of the victim of which the community partook was smeared upon the sacred stone.   "Whatever else was done in connection with a sacrifice," says Robertson Smith, "sprinkling or dashing the blood against the

[1] Lact. i. 20.   D. H. ii. 74.

altar, or allowing it to flow on the ground at its base, was hardly ever omitted." The smearing of the image with blood or fat seems then to date from the time when it was not yet distinguished from the altar. We may suppose that the altar was first simply a spot at which some magical influence seemed to show itself. Sir Alfred Lyall refers, with great probability, the reverence for stocks and stones to "that simple awe of the unusual which belongs to no particular religion." If we may draw an inference from the actual course of religious development in India to-day, the more imaginative devotee justifies the adoration paid to the magical object by attributing it to some spirit or deity. "Yet it seems certain that among the vulgar there is no second meaning in their adoration."[1]

Another kind of altar was made of fresh-cut turf. This was used as a hearth. The kindling of fire was once accomplished with a difficulty which we can scarcely realise in these days, except, perhaps, in France, where the matches, being a government monopoly, are rather worse than the old tinder-box. Hence the places where fire was lit were regarded as more or less sacred. The feeling, too, was long retained that all flame which was not kindled according to the ancient prescription was uncanny. The altar of fresh-cut turf seems then to be the descendant of the space in the open fields at which

[1] Lyall, *Asiatic Studies*, 9 ff.

the new fire was got. At Callender, in Perthshire, all the boys used to meet on the moors upon the first of May, which they called Beltane Day. They cut a circular trench in the ground of such circumference as to hold the company; the round green turf in the middle forming the table. They kindle a fire, apparently on this circular space, and dress a repast at it. Here the sanctity of the altar is, so to speak, artificial. It is due to the act of kindling the magical element, fire. Out of the reverence paid to fire obtained in the right, that is to say the traditional, manner, there grew up the elaborate practices connected with the family hearth and the worship of Vesta. It must have been a great innovation when the dwelling was made to include the hearth. We can overhear the awful warnings held out by the people of the old school, whose fireplaces had always been separated from the dwelling.[1] We may distinguish, then, between the fire altar or hearth, and the altar at which victims were sacrificed.

That the altar is of greater antiquity than the temple, is shown by the fact that important worships often had for their local centre an altar and nothing more; the great altar of Hercules in the cattle market for instance. When temples began to be erected, the altar of sacrifice still remained in the open, while the temple only contained the sacred

[1] Hor. *Carm.* iii. 8, 4. *Gent. Mag.* Superst. 51.

hearth. At Nemi the great altar of sacrifice stood at the north-east corner of the temple of Diana. It was circular, and stood upon a circular base, three steps in height. A stone gutter carried away the blood of the victims.

Roman legends spoke of a time when as yet there were no *images* of the gods. For one hundred and seventy years after the foundation of the city, the Romans, it was declared, continued to build temples and shrines ; but they neither painted nor carved the figure of any of their deities. So Plutarch says, and he gives as the reason the influence of Pythagoras. But if the Romans had not as yet learnt how to portray their gods in marble or on frescoes, they did not leave them without material embodiments. Jove was believed to be present in the flint which they kept in the temple dedicated to him as *Feretrius.* Mars, or perhaps Quirinus, the spear god, was in the spears of Praeneste, and in that which the herald hurled into the enemy's country at the beginning of a war. Vesta was the fire itself. The spirit had scarcely freed itself from the wonder-working talisman, and the primitive mode of viewing the magical object continued side by side with the higher. So the Brahman explains that the black stones marked like ammonites, which some Hindus worship, are really manifestations of Vishnu, while Siva is embodied in the black agate. But the flint, the spear, and the fire were reverenced before it was found that they belonged to Jupiter, or Mars, or Vesta. It was the pontiffs, and those who tried to patch the national customs into a show of reason, who carried out this process of explanation.[1]

The Roman standards consisted at first of a wisp of hay wound round a pole. This must have been a talisman by which the troops were protected. It is instructive to find this replaced by an emblem consciously referred to the chief deity of Rome. This change could only have been possible when the older symbol had lost its magical power. Marius, in his reforms of the Roman military system, replaced the wisp of hay by a silver eagle, the symbol of Jove. These eagles were worshipped by the legions as their guardian spirits, *propria numina* ; and during foreign service they were kept in a small shrine, while in time of peace they were put in the temple of the seed spirit, Saturnus. It is reasonable to suppose that they succeeded to the adoration paid to the older manipular standard.[2]

It must have already occurred to the reader that the objects offered for the adoration of the Roman were exceedingly numerous. The traveller passing along a country road in Latium, would have his fancies touched by " an altar wreathed with flowers, a cave hung with garlands, or an oak tree laden with

---

[1] Plut. *Numa*, 8.   M. Williams, *Hinduism*, 171.   Lyall, *Asiatic Stud.* 10.

[2] Tac. *Ann.* ii. 17.

the horns of cattle, or a hill marked by a fence as sacred, or a log rough-hewn into shape, or an altar of turf smoking with libations, or a stone anointed with oil." But they were not venerated always because they were sacred to some god. They inspired awe, and the feeling was satisfied by some story through which they were connected with some god. The enclosure in which the razor and grindstone were buried, never attained this dignity. This single instance is enough to show that the reference to a deity is not indispensable.[1]

From this assemblage of sacred objects there gradually rise into prominence the altar and the image. It has been suggested that the stone pillar develops into the marble image, while the sacred tree or log is fashioned into the image of wood. The images of the divine ancestors of Latinus were of old cedar wood. Vertumnus was represented by a log of maple roughly hewn into shape.[2]

If we may judge from the use of the word *pater*, along with the names of Roman deities, they were thought of as like men of mature years. It must have somewhat shocked their worshippers when the Greek artist portrayed Father Mars or Father Liber under the youthful forms of an Ares or Dionysus. It seemed as if this were due to pure caprice on the part of the artist. The complaint was made:[3] "We make acquaintance with the gods under such

---

[1] Apul. *Florid.* i. 1.   [2] R. Smith, *Rel. Sem.* 187.   [3] Cic. *N. D.* i. 81.

forms as pleases the painters and sculptors," a charge that might have been brought by a Roman Catholic against the painters of the Italian Renaissance. Who shall say how far the grace of Raphael's Madonnas contributed to impress the gracious figure of the Virgin upon the Italian heart?

After making all deductions, it still remains true that the worship of images is an advance upon that of fetishes, of stocks and stones. "The images of gods and heroes," says Seneca, "are of great assistance to the mind by acting as spurs to the imagination," *incitamenta animi*. The human traits of his deities caused the worshipper to transfer to them the moral consciousness which he felt more and more within his own breast. We must be careful, however, not to project the ideas of these later days to the ages before the fetish had developed into the image. The hymns of the Veda, we are told, contain no indications that the gods were worshipped under any visible presentment. But it must be replied, the worship was paid directly to the element, and not to its personification. Varuna was the sky itself; Agni, like Vesta, the flame; Indra, the rain-cloud. And in like manner the praise which the Pythagoreans of the empire awarded to those early Romans who worshipped their gods without making use of images, is based on a misconception.[1]

We must continually bear in mind the diversity

<hr>

[1] Sen. *Ep.* 64.

of temper and education with which these sacred objects were approached. At the lowest stage comes the man who views all worship as magical in its effects, and for whom there is no hint of spiritual forces in the events which attract his notice. Next, there is the man for whom the acts and circumstances of his ritual are interpreted as the manifestation of spiritual powers. And lastly, there was the cultured pagan, to whom, as Mr. Baring-Gould says, idolatry was impossible. The gods figured in marble and bronze were to him symbols, and nothing more. It is probable that these different temperaments have been found side by side, since ages so remote that, for us, they must be treated as a beginning. There have always been the Peter Bells of religion, for whom all spiritual interpretations are incomprehensible ; the Levites, for whom religion is confined to the ritual and practices with which they are familiar ; and lastly, the rarer natures, for whom nothing is secular.[1]

Not only were the image, the altar, and the temple sacred. This character was attached to every thing that was offered to the gods. A man was guilty of sacrilege at Rome not only if he laid hands upon what in itself was sacred, for instance the image in which the god was manifested, but also if he took down what had been offered, such as the armour affixed to the temple walls. The temple of Diana at

---

[1] *Strange Survivals*, 147.

Nemi was frequented by large numbers of pilgrims, who came to implore the help of the goddess for their ailments, and to pay their vows for the cures she had wrought. Their offerings were hung upon the walls of the shrine, and on other surfaces within the sacred precincts. But the time came when there was no room for more. The priests thereupon removed from the walls the offerings that had become sacred when the goddess accepted them, and buried them in pits, *favissæ*. During the excavations carried on by Lord Savile at Nemi, the workmen, by a stroke of good luck, lighted upon one of these pits, and so furnished him with many of the terra cotta statuettes which are now in the Castle Museum, Nottingham. Alas, the worship of Diana has passed away, like a many other things, good and bad, and no one fears the wrath of the goddess when he handles the offerings of her devotees! In Arabia, in like manner, there was a pit adjoining each sanctuary in which the sacred treasure was stored. It was desired once to lower the ground-level near the Capitoline temple at Rome, in order to set off its dimensions, but the project had to be given up, owing to the cellars and receptacles which were under the surface of the site, in which it was customary to place statues and other sacred objects which it was no longer possible to display in the temple.[1]

The ruin into which the *temples* of Rome fell

---

[1] Cic. *Legg.* ii. 40. R. Smith, *Rel. Sem.* 180. Gell. *N. A.* ii. 10.

during the later Republic, was often pointed at by the later court poets as a token of the national impiety. According to Horace, it was the wickedness of the generation before him that had permitted the temples to fall into ruin, and the images of the gods to become blackened with smoke. This, however, was an exaggeration. The elaboration of the house of the god took place at Rome under Greek influence, and this process was interrupted in the turmoil of the civil wars. For at Rome the temple did not stand in so intimate relation to worship as in Greece. Ovid speaks in a Greek spirit when he says that Augustus had placed the gods under an obligation by repairing their shrines.[1]

"Ancient temples," says Robertson Smith, "are not so much houses where the gods live, as storehouses for the vessels and treasuries of the sanctuary." Hence we may expect their earliest form to be the same as that of the dwelling. Mr. Baring-Gould has collected some very interesting data which prove the wide distribution of what he calls the beehive dwelling. It is found in places as far apart as "the desert of Beersheba and the dunes of Brittany, the Hebrides, the Cornish peninsula, and the Pyrenees." The primitive Roman dwelling also was a round hut; constructed with walls of wood and straw and a thatched roof. Such a hut was maintained on the eastern slope of the Palatine Hill. It was called the

---

[1] Hor. *Carm.* iii. 6. Ovid, *Fasti*, ii. 62.

Hut of Romulus, *casa Romuli.* This was entrusted to the care of certain priests, who preserved it as far as possible in its original state. If, however, in course of time it suffered any harm through storms or otherwise, they carefully patched it up. Some English customs seem to throw light on this Roman one. "On two of the most conspicuous eminences of the forest of Wolmer," says Gilbert White, "stand two arbours or bowers made of the boughs of oak; the one called Waldon Lodge, the other Brimstone Lodge; these the keepers renew annually on the feast of St. Barnabas, taking the old materials for a perquisite. The farm called Blackmoor, in this parish is obliged to find the posts and brushwood for the former. While the farms at Greatham in rotation furnish for the latter, and are all enjoined to cut and deliver the materials at the spot. This custom I mention, because I look upon it to be of very remote antiquity." A hut is sometimes built near the Maypole, as the dwelling of the May-queen. In Bohemia a similar hut is used in the spring, as the court house of the king of the May. It would be interesting to know what purposes were served by the hut of Romulus. This question, however, does not concern us here. We have merely to note that it was regarded as sacred.[1]

The tomb of Caecilia Metella and the Castle of St.

---

[1] *Rel. Sem.* 180. Baring-Gould, *Strange Survivals*, 77. Mannhardt, *A. F. W.* i. 187, 315.

Angelo exhibit the same outward form, but in a dress of stone. As if to render the resemblance complete, there is little doubt that they too were originally covered with a conical roof. Thus the dwelling of the dead was like that of the living.[1]

When we pass from the tomb, and the hut of Romulus, to the temple, we still find circular buildings ; and these are apparently connected with the most primitive worships. The circular shrine in which Vesta was reverenced is of the same form with the home of the prehistoric Roman, and we may reasonably suppose that it was derived from that humble source. It would appear that this building exhibits to us the transition from the dwelling to the sanctuary ; although consecrated, it was not a temple in the technical sense. The temple of Fortune at Praeneste was also of the same shape. We may presume that the round opening in the dome of the Pantheon was repeated in these other buildings of the same kind. It was suggested on a previous page, that the opening in the temple roof gave the worshipper an opportunity of making his vows under the clear sky. This may have been the interpretation put upon an architectural detail. It seems reasonable, however, to see here a kind of chimney. The smoke of the sacred hearth escaped by this means into the open. Further, the chimney itself, although it may have taken its rise in simple

---

[1] Baum. *Denkm.* ill. 665, 666.

necessity, gained probably in the end an almost religious meaning. Just as the augurs were forbidden to have a lid to their lanterns, so the roof of the dwelling must not be entirely covered in. This feeling may perhaps account for the court which forms a characteristic feature of the later Roman house.[1]

Vitruvius credits the Tuscans with the invention of the round temple. There seems, however, to be no adequate evidence to prove this. His statement is an instance of the manner in which the Roman antiquarians at one time credited Etruria with every Roman art, just as at another time everything was traced to a Greek origin. There is justification, however, for attributing the great temple of Jupiter, on the Capitoline Hill, to Etruscan influence. This was completed in the first years of the republic. The style of the building differed from the contemporary Greek manner by its lighter construction and the greater use of wood. Vitruvius, in describing the Tuscan style, lays down a plan in which there are three aisles, the central one being wider than the sides in the proportion of four to three. The wide spacing of the columns made it necessary to form the entablature of wood. This was ornamented with figures of terra cotta and of bronze. Of course the whole edifice was decorated in colour.[2]

The Tuscan plan was modified in the later years

---

[1] Gell. *N. A.* xiv. 7.   [2] Vitruvius, iii. 2 ; iv. 7.

of the Republic under Greek influence. But the plan of the Roman temple differed in several important particulars from the Greek. The external colonnade was rarely carried round all four sides. The Capitoline temple had three rows of columns along the front, a single row on either side, and none at the back. Sometimes there were columns standing free along the front only, as in the temple of Saturn in the forum. The hall of the temple, too, was shorter in proportion to its width than in the Greek examples. The temple of Concord was even narrower from front to back than from side to side. It is far from being true, then, that the Roman temple was a copy merely of the Greek. In fact, the Greeks themselves imitated, in later times, the round temple which was so characteristic of Rome.

The temple was not only like a church in its sacred character. It combined with this the functions both of a bank and a museum. The State treasure of the Republic was kept in the temple of Saturn. The thief thus became guilty both of robbery and of sacrilege. The votive offerings and the sacred vessels made the temple a treasure house, even in those cases in which it was not formally employed for this purpose. To some extent, then, the Roman temple might be compared to the Greek for its artistic interest. It, too, was filled with statues and paintings, with armour taken from an enemy, and with the gifts of the devout. Or to take another illustration, it was like the great churches of mediaeval towns, round which gathered the intellectual interests of the locality, as well as its religious emotions. The vergers acted as guides to the treasures, pointing out their value and meaning. Some of the anecdotes which diversify the study of Roman origins are due to the imagination of these humble "makers" or poets; if we may apply this lofty title to all those who exercise the creative imagination. The ancient guide, like his modern successor, is omniscient, and where he does not remember, he invents "the true stories" which he recounts. The poverty of the Roman mythology is largely due to the dull fancy of the Roman sexton, while the ample fund of legend and anecdote which at first or second hand was gathered by Pausanias into his *Guide to Greece*, came largely from a like, but richer, source.

The gable of the temple was regarded as especially sacred. Private citizens were not permitted to employ this method of finishing a roof. It was one of the chief marks of Caesar's elevation above his fellow citizens that he was allowed to build a gable. If the gable was brought in from Etruria for the purposes of temple building, we can understand the sanctity which attached to it. His residence was thus marked out as of a sacred character.[1]

[1] Cic. *Phil.* ii. 110.

The sanctity of the Roman temple was indicated specially in many other ways. Wreaths of corn ears were hung on the doors of Ceres. The approach to the shrine of the Good Goddess was hung with purple ribbons, and there were long branches of poplar on the temple walls.[1] Another, and less pleasing custom, was to put the skulls of the slaughtered victims along the frieze, and to unite them with garlands. A trace of this has remained in the carving often employed to adorn the Tuscan order, with exquisite lack of propriety. The head of the animal was believed to contain its life, and so the skull of the animal became a kind of talisman, protecting the building from harm. In the Market Place of Cologne there is an attic window, from which two horses seem to be looking. The reason is said to be that, in 1357, two horses walked right upstairs into the garret. They were got down again with some difficulty, and their heads were stuffed and put there in remembrance of the marvel. When Mr. Baring-Gould inspected them, he found them to be of wood. This story reminds one of the Roman stories of the cattle that go upstairs. Two of these are told with every circumstance of time and place. We are impelled to enquire whether they may not have had an origin like that of Cologne; whether the heads of both horses and cattle were not fixed upon a building as magical safeguards.

[1] Prop. V. ix. 27.

For a new building does require some protection. It is still found that new, and especially unfinished, houses, are subject to inexplicable noises of rapping and the like.[1]

When the foundations of the great temple were dug, a human head of perfect preservation was found by the workmen.[2] It is more than likely that it was put there intentionally. The belief that human life must be sacrificed, in order to make sure the foundations of a building, is very widely spread. Even if it is not given voluntarily, there is still no escape. Hiel, the Bethelite, laid the foundations of Jericho with the loss of Abiram his firstborn, and set up the gates thereof with the loss of his youngest son, Segub. The story of the death of Remus hints at a like sacrifice when the walls of the Roman city were built. The victim (who was probably not called Remus), lost his life in order that atonement might be made to the spirits whom the new building disturbed. The spirit of the man thus killed became a ghost and haunted the place, if we may apply the language of the present. Were the Lares the spirits of the men killed, when the city was built? We may compare this idea with that which seems to underlie the devotion of the Decii. Many peoples of the present are still dominated

---

[1] Baring-Gould, *Strange Survivals*, 37. Lang, in *Class. Rev.* vii. 453. Livy, xxi. 62 ; xxxvi. 37.
[2] *Supra*, p. 149.

by it. In 1860 the king of Burmah, father of Theebaw, built Mandalay. Fifty-three persons were then buried alive, three under each of the twelve gates, one under each of the palace gates, and four under the throne itself. This usage seems to have left some traces at Rome, and must be taken account of in explaining the origin of Roman beliefs.[1]

[1] 1 *Kings*, xvi. 34. *Strange Survivals*, 35.

THE DIVINE VICTIM

JUST as in the land certain places are marked off as sacred in a special degree, so is it in the community. Out of the sacred character which attaches to it as a whole, there emerge into prominence the special sanctities of the father, the king, the priest, and, in a sense that will appear shortly, the god.

The position of the father in the Roman family, his authority, in theory unlimited, over his children, seems to receive explanation when it is viewed in the light of Roman beliefs. Not only were his children indebted to him for their birth; they were also beholden to him for the continuance of their life. Plutarch asks why the Romans, in ancient times, never went out to supper without taking their young sons with them, even when they were still quite young children. The same explanation of this, perhaps, may be given as of the *couvade*. The life of the young boy is bound up with that of his father, and his life is protected by nearness to his father. There is a sympathy like that which causes the father to be tended carefully, in some parts of the world, for some time after the birth of his child. More than this, certain offices could only be filled by those whose father was still alive; as, for instance, the chief place among the ancient body of heralds. In the priestly character which attached to the Roman father, we may notice that he did not derive his sanctity from this office. It was his sanctity rather that marked him out for it. Whether he made offerings at the family hearth to the fire spirit, or to the guardian spirits of the home, or to the good spirits at the family sepulchre, or at the boundaries of his farm to the boundary spirits, he performed acts which in part owed their efficacy to his own qualities as the depositary of the family life.[1]

There were priestly colleges at Rome, and there were special priesthoods; but there was no priestly order. No strict line was drawn, such as separates the Brahman from the other castes, or the priest from the laity in Roman Catholic countries. For the head of each family was himself possessed of a status almost sacerdotal. Hence there was no need of special intermediaries between him and the gods. And this still held of the citizen when he became a magistrate. The colleges of the pontiffs, of the augurs, of the fifteen, and of the seven, were called in at his discretion. They might not give

[1] Plut. R. Q. 62.

their advice unasked. They were his assistants in acts wherein he himself was the chief agent. There are other indications of the priority enjoyed by the religion of the family. Even the highest college of all, the pontiffs, could not make innovations there. When Roman society was shaken to its depths by the affair of the Bacchanalia, the Senate did not dare to interfere with such private celebrations as could not be interrupted without giving rise to religious scruple. Further, considerable freedom was permitted in the formation of new religious societies. These might have common funds, a master of ceremonies, and their own priest. Provided that the new rites did not interfere with the due observance of the old, and that no breach of order took place, an uneasy or superstitious conscience could seek rest in the new worships with which the Romans came into contact in Greece, Asia, Syria, or in Egypt. Thus the influence of the priestly colleges was limited in two directions. On the one hand were the ancestral worships of the family, on the other the incoming worships of the surrounding nations. Since, then, the citizen took precedence of the priest, Roman religion was guided and controlled by the considerations of statesmanship. The foreign and the internal policies of Rome were governed by practical motives alone, to the exclusion of those more romantic purposes which illumine the history of some of the Greek states, or of mediaeval Europe. There is, it is true, an important exception to this assertion. The conflict of the patricians and the plebeians had in its earlier stages a religious colour. Yet there is, perhaps, no more need to attribute entire sincerity to the party that used religious considerations as a cloak, than to those who took the leading part in opposing the admission of Dissenters to the House of Commons.

The most ancient priesthoods seem to have been hereditary. This was the case, doubtless, in many instances where the State took over the worship which had previously been that of a single family alone. Thus the Luperci were chosen from the families of the Fabii and the Quinctilii. The worship of Hercules, at the great altar, was originally a family worship of the Potitii and Pinarii. It is possible that the name of the Flaminian clan is derived from the name of one of the special priesthoods. We can trace a similar transition from private to public worship in Israel. The children of Dan sent for the priest of the house of Micah. " And they carried off the gods which Micah had made, the graven image, the teraphim, and the molten image. And they said unto him, Is it better for thee to be priest unto the house of one man, or to be priest unto a tribe and a family in Israel?" It is not impossible that a priesthood may have been hereditary, even when it involved the death of the holder. In Bengal there used to be a noble family, which held its domains by surrendering one of its number to be killed by the sabre of the king. In course of time the ceremonial was modified. The man fell beneath the sword, but it was merely a feint, and the victim of the sham decapitation reappeared three days after, giving it out that he had come forth from the tomb. A like severity of ancient customs seems to have left traces at Rome. The clan of the Manlii at Rome avoided giving the name of Marcus to any son born in the clan. We may infer from this that the possession of the name was once thought to be bound up with evil consequences. Marcus signified, probably, Mars' man, or sacred to Mars. The early Romans, who attached such extreme importance to names, must have had special rules to guide them in the use of the *praenomina*. The legend which explained the avoidance of this name was incorporated into the annals of Rome. It was said that Marcus Manlius, who was surnamed Capitolinus, was on guard in the citadel on the Capitoline Hill, when he was aroused by the clamour of the sacred geese. This was just in time for him to raise the alarm, and to repel a scaling party of the Gauls, who at the time were in possession of the rest of Rome. Subsequently, the story went on, he was found guilty of trying to establish a monarchy, and was put to death by being thrown from the Capitoline Rock. If we suppose that he held one of the priesthoods which brought with them kingly attributes, we find an explanation of most of the circumstances. On the one hand, it would account for the charge brought against him of attempting to make himself king. On the other, it is possible that some superstition was satisfied by his death. Some half-forgotten custom suggested that he should be offered as a sacrifice to Jupiter by being thrown from the Tarpeian Rock.[1] We shall see, shortly, that the priest was also the sacrifice, according to some ancient usages. If it was a family custom to devote to the priesthood those only of its members who were named Marcus, the later taboo becomes comprehensible.

The exact truth of the case is probably beyond attainment. We are, therefore, left to hypotheses. Was Manlius the Flamen of Jupiter? As priest of the great temple, he would also have charge of the sacred geese. If he took advantage in any way of the kingly attributes which attached to this priesthood; if, in particular, he released the debtors who were in chains, we can understand the alarm which such action would arouse.[2] The rights of the Flamen, in this respect, are paralleled by mediaeval customs. "According to the Chronicle of Evesham, it appears that in 1364 the Abbot of Battel, going towards London, met a felon condemned to the gallows in the King's Marshalsea, and in virtue of his prerogatives, liberated him from death. And although the King

---

[1] *Judges*, xviii. Reclus, *Prim. Folk*, 308. Livy, vi. 20.
[2] *Supra*, p. 147.

and other magnates took much offence at the act, yet, upon plea, he had his charter confirmed."[1] Some of the restrictions which limited the freedom of the Flamen Dialis seem to be due to the fear that he would abuse his position in the same way that Manlius is said to have done. In fact, the office was intentionally degraded.[2]

But the priest of Jupiter was more than the holder of certain royal prerogatives. He was himself possessed of special magical virtues. When the transition was made from animism; when, as we may imagine, the medicine-man became the priest of the tribal deity; his powers were attributed, not to himself, but to the indwelling of the god. Indeed he was, in a certain sense, the incarnation of the god. So the Roman general, on the day of his triumph, wore a tunic embroidered with palm branches and victories, and a toga embroidered with gold upon a purple ground. He carried a sceptre, on which an eagle sat. Over his head there was held a golden crown of oak-leaves set with precious stones. All these ornaments were borrowed from the statue of the god in the great temple. Moreover, the countenance of the general was painted with vermilion, in the same way as was done to the god on feast days. The god, then, was believed to have manifested himself in the victory of the Roman troops. So, too, when the games were held, the god

<hr>

[1] Lower, *Chronicles of Battel Abbey*, 204.   [2] Livy, xxvii. 8.

himself came down from the Capitol in the person of the praetor, who was attired like the triumphing general.   It was, then, as the embodiment of Jupiter, of the oak spirit, that the Flamen was regarded. Hence he was forbidden to touch, or even name, ivy.

We find little in all this that answers to the inspiration of a priest or a prophet by a divine presence.   There was no order of prophets who claimed to be the mouthpieces of heaven, like the rishis of Hinduism; who caught the eternal word, or saw the sacred message written by the hand of a god.   The story of Numa conversing with Jupiter is a later invention.   Virgil's description of the inspiration of the priestess of Apollo, rises far beyond the levels upon which the Roman imagination moved. Holiness and the prophetic power were almost physical properties, which marked out certain men, and even things; the Lots of Praeneste, for instance. The profound thought that the personality of man may be the vehicle of the will of a divine being, was first brought to Rome by the systems, half philosophical, half theological, which came into favour at the end of the Republic.

The traditional history of the Roman monarchy is made up largely of legends invented to account for various institutions.   It is generally admitted that, taken as a whole, this history is unreliable.   A sharp line is drawn, however, at the expulsion of Tarquin, as though trustworthy records began from 509 B.C. If we may judge from parallel examples elsewhere, and by the indirect evidence afforded in the status of the Flamen Dialis and the king of worship, the transformation of Rome from a monarchy into a republic was gradual. The king was successively deposed from being the actual into the titular, and then into the ritual head of the State. He gave way before his magistrates in the same way as the Mikado of Japan yielded for a time to the Tycoon, the Merovingian kings of France to the mayors of the palace. To take two points in which this history of the end of the monarchy is open to criticism : the struggle which was necessary before the Etruscan kings could be driven out seems to have been far more intense than we should gather at first view from the annals ; the story of the flight of Tarquin was told to explain the *regifugium*, of which, how-ever, quite a different account is to hand. It is reasonable to suppose that the foreign dynasty, which ruled *de facto*, was content to allow those whom they dispossessed, to exercise their ritual functions.[1]

It is a curious fact that the Flamen Dialis and the king of worship retained many marks of a royal station. The Flamen was by right a member of the Senate. More than this, he had the curule chair and other insignia, which marked the highest offices in

[1] Mommsen, *R. H.* i. 330.

the State, and were almost certainly derived from the surroundings of the monarch. With the exception of the king of worship, he had the highest place at all banquets. He seems to have been chosen by the same ceremonies as that other high officer. The Romans themselves were struck by his royal character, and his duties were said to have been performed by King Numa, when as yet there were no other priesthoods. If he was the successor of the monarch as far as his priestly duties went, we can understand certain precautions which were taken to prevent his resuming the other prerogatives. He was forbidden to see the citizens girt for battle, outside the walls. In the same way, the king of worship was forbidden to exercise any magistracy, and to address any public meetings of the citizens. The royal ceremonies by which he was chosen are described by Livy. His chief duties consisted in certain sacrifices to Janus, and in announcing the festivals of each month. He was conjoined with the Flamen Dialis in providing the wool which the pontiffs used in certain rites of purification. This fact, and the resemblance between the position of the king of worship and the Flamen, lead to the supposition that the duties of both were performed once by the king of Rome. This was the case, at any rate, with Numa; if, that is, we may follow popular legends. There would seem, then, to have been a distribution of the priestly functions of the king, analogous to that of his political functions. As consul, praetor, and censor divided the latter, so the king of worship and the Flamen Dialis divided the religious duties between them. But we are not informed how the change was effected.[1]

There were priest kings in other Latin towns. We learn of them as holding office at Lanuvium, Tusculum, and Bovillae. The most interesting case is the king of the wood at Aricia; upon whose sacred charge Mr. Frazer has founded the arguments of *The Golden Bough*. The Arician priest was attached to the temple of Diana, and obtained his office by the slaughter of his predecessor. In expectation of a like attack from another ruffian, he was armed always. The mad emperor Gaius, thinking that the contemporary priest had held his office too long, sent down against him a picked adversary. Let us trace the steps by which the voluntary self-sacrifice of the king degenerated into the bribing of a runaway to hold the priesthood at the risk of his neck.[2]

According to the ancient Norse belief, there was a great tree called the horse of Odin, or Yggdrasil, and this tree supported heaven and earth. In this tree Odin hangs himself for nine days and nights, and in his tortures he sings to himself an ancient song, of which the words have come down :

> " I know that I hung on the tree shaken by the wind nine
>   live-long nights,
> Pierced by the spear, holy to Odin, holy to myself."

[1] Livy, i. 20. Gell. xv. 27. Plut. *R. Q.* 63. Ovid, *Fasti*, ii. 22.
[2] Strabo, v. 239. Suet. *Gaius*, 35. Wilm. 1326, 1757, 1773.

The god is, in many other cases, the victim as well. There is a text in the Brahmanas which runs, " The lord of creatures offered himself a sacrifice for the gods."[1]

The gallows was indeed at first a tree, as the name of a street in Leicester shows, Gallowtree Gate ; and it was regarded as sacred to Odin. The belief in the world tree grew out of the belief in the sacredness of those trees which, according to the popular notion, had an influence upon the crops and herds of the villagers. The hanging on the gallows answers to the offering of a human victim to the tree spirit, or as we may say, it binds the life of the tree to that of the community through the victim. Strange as these ideas may seem to us, they were part of the system of ideas in which the primitive mind moved. Even the human beings on whom fell the melancholy lot of sacrifice, accepted the stern office without resentment. We must not regard these usages, therefore, as simple cruelty done by the tribe to one of its members. If we may judge by the stories of Curtius and the Decii, the office of victim was sought rather than shunned. So, too, the example of Odin found royal imitators. To die for his people was a lofty, though awful, privilege of the monarch. The idea of substitution was familiar to Virgil. " One life shall be given for many," he sings. An instance is recorded in the Heimskringla of a king named Olaf, who was

---

[1] B.-Gould, *Strange Survivals*, 239. M. Williams, *Hinduism*, 36.

dedicated to Odin upon the occurrence of bad harvests. Another king hanged himself upon the gallows, of his own free-will, as an offering to Odin. Who can tell what inducements were held out in those earliest days to the man who died for the people? Did the popular voice promise a life of everlasting bliss to the ancient king of the wood, when he was slaughtered at the foot of his holy tree? Or was it that he was thought to become a god by the very act of immolation? This last is a very probable explanation.

If the victim becomes divine in the act of sacrifice, the form of his death will be attributed to the spirit whom he represents. Hence in some cases we may argue from the legends of the god's death, to the form of the sacrifices said to be made to him. We may suppose that the priests who represented Dionysus were torn asunder by wild horses, rent in pieces by the worshippers, or thrown into the sea. The death of Heracles on Mount Oeta was enacted in grim earnest on Greek mountain peaks, and may have had its prototype in sacrifices such as those of the Jews in the valley of Hinnom. Just as the Greek god was burnt on the hill-top, so the contemporaries of Jeremiah built the high places of Baal to burn their sons in the fire for burnt offerings unto Baal.

A mode of human sacrifice, which was practised till quite recently among the Khonds, throws light upon the ideas which we are considering. The human victim, *meriah* or mediator, was regarded as the embodiment of the deity Tari, and, before the sacrifice, she was worshipped as such. On the eve of the solemnity, she was washed and arrayed in new clothes. She was then taken from door to door, and led away into the forest. A pole, thirty or forty feet high, was raised. This was wreathed with flowers, and surmounted by a peacock's head. There she was bound, and left until the following day. When the appointed hour came, a potion of opium was given to stupefy her, in order that she might not seem to struggle against the doom awaiting her. The priest struck the first blow, and then all the crowd rushed upon her, rending her piecemeal in order that they might participate severally in the virtues of her flesh and blood. When, in the years 1848–1852, the government of India took measures to end this savage practice, the Khond theologians saw the force of the arguments which could be brought against human sacrifice, especially when they were supported by the British troops. It appeared that the goddess could be represented by an animal, as well as by a human being.[1]

When it was not possible to find persons offering themselves for sacrifice, they were taken by compulsion ; the lot being used to indicate those who were acceptable to the god, *or to the lot itself.* Captives taken in war, strangers, and criminals, were welcome substitutes for the lives of citizens. When

---

[1] Reclus, *Prim. Folk,* 320.

the Germans defeated Varus, they slaughtered their captives as offerings to Odin, and the avenging army which Germanicus led, found the heads of their countrymen hanging upon the sacred trees. In the West of England there are fields which go by the name of Gallowstraps, about which the people say that whoever sets foot upon them is destined for the gibbet. Mr. Baring-Gould suggests that this belief grew out of the custom of setting certain spots aside as sacred, and sacrificing to the god those who un-wittingly set foot upon them. The Romans buried four foreigners alive in the forum in historical times. It is noteworthy also that the king of the wood was a stranger.[1]

It seems paradoxical, at first sight, to include criminals among holy persons. We find many indications, however, of their sacred character. The criminal hanged upon a tree, among the Israelites, was said to be "the curse of God." It appears, however, that the human beings so killed were regarded as offerings. When the Gibeonites took the sons of Saul, "they hanged them in the hill before the Lord." In ancient Germany the priests, alone, had the office of punishing criminals, "As though," Tacitus says, "it was by command of the god." At Rome the eighth of the Twelve Tables said: "If a patronus is guilty of fraud towards a client let him be accursed," *sacer*, literally sacred.

[1] Tac. *Ann.* i. 61. *Strange Survivals*, 242.

A contemporary decree of the people explains this sacred character, when it consecrates to Jupiter the life of any man who did violence to the tribunes. By the laws of the Twelve Tables, further, the corn thief, if he was an adult, was hanged as an offering to Ceres. In this way human sacrifice was kept up at Rome long after it, apparently, had ceased; just as in England, to this day, murderers expiate their crime on what, by strict and uninterrupted descent, is the tree of Odin. If, then, the criminal was one who had broken a tribal rule, or had trespassed upon the dues of a tribal deity, the gravity of his wrong-doing was not measured primarily either by his intention, or by the actual amount of his act; it was referred to the harm which might thereby come upon his countrymen. Hence, the apparent severity of ancient codes. They looked away from the criminal altogether. The sin of Achan was not great in itself, but in the opinion of the Hebrew chronicler it caused the defeat of his countrymen, and was but inadequately recompensed by the stoning of the criminal, and the burning of "his sons and his daughters, and his oxen, and his asses, and his sheep."[1]

We may infer, then, that the death of the king of the wood was but an isolated survival of many rites in which human sacrifice played a leading part. Nor shall we be surprised to find that, in later times,

[1] Pliny, *N. H.* xviii. 12.   *Joshua*, vii. 24.

such immolation was limited to the guilty who had been convicted before a civil tribunal, or to the innocent who chose to die as a voluntary sacrifice. The voluntary immolation seems to be the most ancient type of all, while the execution of a criminal is a survival from the latest type. Even in 97 B.C. the Roman government found it necessary to prohibit human sacrifice.[1]

It appears that human sacrifice may leave its traces in the manner by which criminals are executed. Hence we may argue, sometimes, from the punishment to its origin. A guilty vestal virgin was buried alive. This was an ancient form of sacrifice, as appears from the story of the burial of the Greeks and Gauls in the forum. The vestal virgins then, may have once been victims set aside for the service of the fire spirit, with a view to being offered to him. The office, it appears, was one to be shunned. Not more than one fire maiden was "taken" from a single family, and the office of flamen, augur, etc., excused the daughter of its holder.[2]

The flamens and the augurs also were said to be "taken," in sacrificial language, as though by an act in which they themselves had no voice. The curious story of a man who was made Flamen Dialis against his will, shows that the office was not always voluntarily undertaken in later times. It was surrounded by elaborate restrictions which may have arisen, in

---

[1] Mommsen, *R. H.* i. 181 ; iii. 438.   [2] Gell. i. 12.

part, from his liability to be made a sacrifice, like those which the Khonds observed with the meriahs, or the Mexicans with their human victims, or the Carthaginians with the children whom they set aside for offering to the king, Moloch. It is not necessary to suppose that the vestals, or the augurs, or the flamens, were viewed at any time as doomed to inevitable sacrifice. But as depositaries, or channels of divine influence, they were marked out for such an end, if the interests of the community seemed to demand unusual measures, either of precaution or of remedy. Hence the rules by which their sacred character was preserved inviolate, were also the rules by which they were kept fit for sacrifice.

Other rules by which the flamen was governed may have had an historical origin, such as we have seen in the case of Manlius. Other rules again, perhaps those which relate to his food, may have been caste rules, like those of the higher caste Hindus. In later times, however, the original meaning of these restrictions was lost, and they were regarded as curious merely, when they were not felt as burdensome. In the light of these various considerations, it may be possible to trace the sources of many of the numerous particulars given by Plutarch and Gellius.

So far as any conscious purposes can be discerned in them, they seem to be directed against the possibility of pollution in the sense already defined, and also against any enchantments which might entrap the soul of the sacred individual, or separate him from the city, of which, in some dim sense, he was one of the safeguards.

Originally the flamen was not permitted to be a single night away from Rome; such absence being accounted "impious." Yet within the bounds of Rome his spirit must be allowed to go free. We have seen that he might not employ a knot in his clothing, and all rings that he wore had to be broken. In order that even in sleep he should not be severed from the city soil, the feet of his couch were smeared with mud. Another might not sleep there, and he was further protected from evil by charms at the head of his bed, namely, a bag containing iron and straw. Since his life was especially resident in his head, many precautions were taken to guard it. His hair might not be cut by one who was not a member of the community. He might not anoint himself in the open, and when he was out of doors he always wore the *apex* or cap, with a small wooden spike at the top wound round with wool. The cap was made of the wool of the white thick-fleeced wethers, *altilanei*, which were sacrificed to Jupiter. The spike was taken from some "lucky" tree, so that the life of the priest was put under its protection. His hair and nails were buried under the same tree.[1]

[1] Gell. x. 15. Plut. *R. Q.* 40, 44, 50, 109–113.

No one could be chosen as the *flamen* of Jupiter unless he were born of parents whose marriage had been celebrated according to the ancient rite of *confarreatio*. The same regulation applied, doubtless, to his wife, *flaminica*. They must have been married, too, in the same manner. Here, to all appearances, we find an instance of religious conservatism. The innovations to which civil life was exposed, were kept away from the circle of the priesthood as far as possible. Arguing from this, we might conclude that the life of the private citizen was limited at one time by many taboos, like those of the flamen.

In his election, three candidates had to be named with the due qualifications of birth, and the chief pontiff made his selection from them. The ancient marriage rituals fell into disuse with the lapse of time, and in the year 24 A.D. it was impossible to find persons fitted to serve. Provided the traditional requirements were satisfied, the moral character of the candidate was not thought of great moment. In fact, a young man, C. Valerius Flaccus, was chosen flamen, during the second Punic war, precisely because his character was very bad. Livy, inspired by later ideas, was shocked by the apparent impiety, and would have passed over the story in silence, except for its good tendency. Valerius had been careless and dissolute. At last his relatives, in despair, bethought themselves that the strict rules by which the life of a flamen was encompassed might act as a check upon the young rake. The pontiff became an accomplice in the family plot, and Valerius was chosen against his will. However, he surprised everyone by devoting himself to the duties of his office, and commanded the respect of the city to such an extent that he claimed, and succeeded in regaining, the seat in the Senate which was the flamen's by prescription, but had remained unfilled, owing to the mean position of his predecessors.[1]

The election of the flamen took place at a meeting of the people specially summoned, *comitia calata*, at which they did not vote, but came together to hear the will of the gods. The pontiff discovered this by divination. But the Roman magistrates understood already the art of finding the desired omens, as appears from the tale about Valerius. The office thus assigned, ostensibly by the will of heaven, took precedence even of the authority of the father, and the flamen was the only man who escaped from the power of his ascendant.[2]

The Flamens of Mars and Quirinus ranked along with the priest of Jupiter. The same birth qualifications were demanded of them. But they were not bound by restrictions so severe. They even filled the governorships of the provinces. Theoretically the Flamen Dialis might not leave Rome. In practice this rule was not observed, and on such occasions his functions were carried out by the pontiff.

[1] Tac. *Ann.* iv. 16. Livy, xxvii. 8.   [2] Gaius, i. 130.

Human sacrifice may leave its traces in the rules of the priesthood. But there is one particular kind of act which was not so much symbolical of sacrifice, as equivalent to it. The banishment of a citizen, his interdiction from fire and water, was from the point of view of law, his civil death. We may be sure that it was no sentimental repugnance to the shedding of blood which led the Romans to expel a criminal, rather than put him to death. Here, too, the civil act of later times can be traced to the ritual practices of earlier. The banishment of Cicero was one of a continuous series of usages which carries us back to the " sacred spring," in which bands of young citizens, devoted to Mars, used to be driven forth to seek their fortunes outside the national boundaries.

The festival of the twenty-fourth of February or *regifugium*, may indeed date back to the time when the early monarchy was brought to an end. But there was another festival on the twenty-fourth of May, on which the king of worship, so it was believed, acted the flight of Tarquin. After making a sacrifice in the comitium, he fled from the forum. At Delphi, every ninth year, there were special festivals, and on one of these, the Feast of Crowns, ceremonies were performed somewhat like the flight of the king. The explanation given was that they imitated the flight of the god after his battle with the python. In the May festival at Rome, then, we light upon one of those ritual acts which are to be explained by the rules of magic, rather than by reference to an historical event of which they are the memorials. The flight of the king at Rome, and of the god at Delphi, was like the driving out of the scarecrow from English villages. A figure of death was anciently borne by the young men into the villages, from which it was driven by the people who disliked it as an ominous appearance, while some gave them money to remove the *mawkin*.[1] Sometimes the part of the " mawkin " is acted by one of the company, and then the likeness to the antique usages becomes closer. So the old Mars was driven out of the city on the first full moon of the Roman year. The flight of the priest-king seems to have the same meaning as the flight of the god.[2]

The results to which recent investigations in the subject-matter of this chapter are tending, and to which they have led us, may be summarised briefly. The priestly character is at first combined with that of the monarch, and depends upon certain magical attributes inherent in the person of the priest. These attributes are referred to the presence of a divine influence, so that, in a sense, one man is king, priest, and god. Through his death, the communal life is renewed ; the interpretations of this renewal being various. The victim may be killed either to make way for a stronger representative of the god, or—what after all comes to the same thing—he is

---

[1] (?) May King.　　　[2] Plut. *Q. G.* 12. Hampton, i. 234.

supposed to have received pollution and, in being driven away, he carries off the evils of his people. When the notion of an external deity becomes clear, these magical interpretations yield to theological ones. The slaughter or expulsion of the divine priest is thought to be grateful to the god of the nation. It is at this moment of transition that the profound idea seems to have sprung up, that the god was offered to himself in the person of the sacrifice.

THE SACRED DRAMA

WHEN the ceremonial of Rome is considered in its detail, it is found to be a kind of representation of the ends to which it is directed. Just as the pontifical lists enumerated the operations of the husbandman by the names of the corresponding deities, so the acts of Roman ritual prefigured, in a language of gesture, the purposes for which sacrifice was offered. The sacred calendar was a perpetual masque of the seasons, in which the life of the farmer was reflected as in a magic mirror. Through these traditional rites the life of the land, of the trees and corn, of the cattle, and of the citizens themselves, was renewed from time to time, and a limit was set continually to that process of degeneration which never ceased.

When the ceremonial of the holy day was being performed under the eyes of an expectant throng, the very air must have seemed to strain towards the mystic issues of sacrifice. We cannot restore, after all these years, the exquisite and complex emotion which gave and took colour amid the solemn circumstances of worship. It is possible, nevertheless, to sum up the details, and combine their several contributions to the whole effect. We can also mark off those salient distinctions of temper which are often overlooked because of their very prominence, as we try to enter the Roman mind through the portals of our own.

Ancient ritual in Rome, as in Greece and Palestine, was essentially joyous. The ceremonies of worship brought together the citizens in friendly concourse, and added social interests to the deeper excitements of religion. For the poorer classes they furnished the sole occasions on which flesh-meat entered into their diet. Answering to this festal character, the surroundings of sacrifice took upon themselves more and more splendour, as the material wealth of the city increased. So far as this change threw more expense upon the worshipper, it threatened to cut off the national religion at its very root, in the affections of the frugal peasant. But the good sense of the Roman held by the simpler usages of Numa. The poor man, making a scanty gift with his prayers, was as sure of securing the divine favour, as his wealthy countryman. Cicero declares that uprightness is more acceptable than lavish offerings.

It was the privilege of the rich citizen to furnish the means for the seasons of public enjoyment. These, by their frequent occurrence, broke in upon and relieved the monotony and hardship of life at a low level. At Rome nearly every other day was a holy day. Our national history, in its later developments since the Reformation, incapacitates us from understanding this aspect of pagan religions. Mediaeval usages, indeed, brought down the unbroken tradition of religious festivity to the middle of the seventeenth century. Our northern temperament, however, dwarfed and distorted by mistaken views of religion and of life, has lost for a time that capacity for serious and reflecting enjoyment, which is one of the best heirlooms of humanity. In our insular pride and ignorance, we scoff at the festivals of the Roman Church as survivals from Paganism. But, in this respect, the religion of Numa and its Christian successor answer to an intrinsic quality of man's nature, and can be judged by their fruits. The music of Palestrina is as noble as the plantation melodies of Mr. Sankey, and the sculpture of Amiens bears comparison, for spiritual beauty, with those inscriptions upon foundation stones, in which all the expressiveness of our religious edifices is concentrated.

The hilarity of ancient religion is the clue to that strange mixture of devotion and levity, which surprises us in the comedies of Aristophanes, and, to some extent, in Roman religion, as in the absurd story about the charm against thunder, or in the revels of the Lupercalia. While ancient worship was associated with lightness of heart and gaiety, the occasions of amusement took upon themselves a sacred character. *Laetitiam cum divum honore iungunto*, says Cicero ; let worship be combined with rejoicing. Theatrical performances and horse races were counted, along with sacrifice and prayer, as religious exercises. According to Macrobius, there were four kinds of holy solemnity, sacrifice, sacred banquets, public festivals, and games.[1]

If we compare Roman worship with that of Greece, we find that it is characterized by a certain dry formalism, and, therefore, loses somewhat of the brilliant gaiety which the Greeks knew so well how to give to their sacred functions. This formal element of Roman worship may be referred to the national lack of imaginative power. The dry and rigid Roman character was bound by precedent, and adapted itself but slowly to its circumstances. It was suspicious of change, and, in its adherence to the letter, was incapable of apprehending the spirit even of ancient traditions. Much less could it read the meaning of the changing present. This national temperament was reflected in the dull formality of the objects of its worship.

Further, the exercise of the religious imagination was discouraged. Any innovation in the utterances and forms of worship ran the risk of breaking the spells laid by them. To the thinkers of later times this suggested a certain mystic attitude of mind,

[1] Cic. *Legg.* ii. 22.   Macr. *Sat.* i. 16, 4.

than which, however, nothing could have been more alien to the Roman worshippers of early times. Macrobius was mistaken, then, when he explained why it was forbidden to speak of the beliefs inspired by worship. "It is not permitted," he says, "that the secret explanations which flow from the well-spring of pure truth should be divulged, even in the very act of worship." Macrobius speaks here rather in the strain of the later Greek theologians.[1]

The head of the Roman Church takes his title from the supreme rank in the hierarchy of ancient Rome. The chief pontiff, although in precedence he ranked below the Flamen of Jupiter and the king of worship, was, nevertheless, their official superior. We can measure the gap which separates ancient worship from modern faiths by the character of the pontiff's office. It was not his business to inquire into the beliefs held by his fellow citizens, or into the attitude of mind which accompanied their acts of worship. Provided that the prescribed forms were observed both in word and act, he had no further care. There was no need, then, that the pontiff himself should be of any given temper of mind. If he carried out the duties of his office, the State did not concern itself with his private opinions, or even his private character. Sometimes it happened that the holder of the sacred office was a man of untarnished morals, who believed sincerely in the efficacy of his

[1] Macr. *Sat.* i. 7, 18.

ceremonial. Scaevola, of whom Cicero was a disciple, was such a man. He was singled out by Cicero, among all the men of his time, for nobility of character and uprightness. He must have been like the good parish priest in the gay company of the Canterbury pilgrims. But when Caesar succeeded him in the year of the conspiracy of Catiline, the chief pontificate was filled by one whose character, great in so many respects, was anything rather than religious. Much has been made of the words which Sallust puts into his mouth, when the debate was held on the great conspiracy. "Death," he said, "puts an end to all the ills of mankind. Afterwards there is space neither for joy nor tears." It may be questioned, however, whether Caesar is here at variance with his more religious contemporaries. These words of his are echoed in the eternal rest and slumber, of which the inscriptions and the poets speak. The belief in immortality was not a part of the Roman religion, any more than was a moral temper of mind. Even Hezekiah speaks of death in accents like those of Caesar. "Nothingness cannot praise thee, death cannot celebrate thee ; they that go down into the pit, cannot hope for thy truth." Caesar is consistent, then, with himself and with the beliefs of his time when, in the traditional phrases, he swears by the gods as eternal, *immortales*, contrasting them with the mortality of man. His Epicureanism was thus no bar to his becoming chief pontiff. Just as little was he hampered by his wild and dissolute youth. For this had not interfered with his public career, and it was there that duty was most binding upon a Roman. Hence in the eulogy of Sallust, a list of virtues is set forth which may have justified his election in the eyes of citizens generally, although to a modern eye they seem to lack that touch of austerity which the sacerdotal office demands. "Caesar was great," the historian declares, "by his lavish kindness: mildness and pity distinguished him. He was ready to give, to help, to pardon; and his affability encouraged the unfortunate to come to him for refuge. He had schooled himself to long hours of toil, which he devoted to the interests of his friends, often to the damage of his own. Military command and warfare were desired by him as a field in which his characteristic excellences might be displayed." This partisan picture enables us to comprehend how Caesar may have seemed an ideal chief pontiff to his contemporaries. This brilliant man of the world understood also what was expected from a candidate for the supreme office of the Roman priesthood. He lavished, during his canvass, such enormous bribes that, if he failed, ruin would stare him in the face. As he went down into the city upon the morning of his election, he said to his mother as she kissed him, "I shall not come again, unless I come as pontiff." In this respect, too, history has repeated itself." The successor of Innocent VIII. obtained the papal throne by paying his price to each member of the sacred college. Cardinal Sforza was gained over by a gift of silver, which required four mules to carry it into the palace of his eminence.[1]

The hilarious character of ancient worship, and the formal temper of the Romans, led them to some strange consequences. Bearing these in mind, let us now examine, in detail, the different offices of ancient worship, the prayers and vows, the music and dancing, and the sacrifice.

"I remember," says Mr. W. G. Clark, "to have read a lecture of Dr. Newman's, in which he maintained the thesis that the profane and blasphemous oaths habitually used by the people of Italy, proved that the objects of their devotion were always present to their minds, in whatever aspect, and that the state of mind of an Italian was far preferable to the apathy and indifference of the lower orders in England. To this one might reply, on behalf of our countrymen, that their favourite expletive, by the same reason, proves the thought of eternal salvation to be always present to their minds." If this be the test of devotion, it is worth while to enquire why the priest of Jupiter, like St. Eligius, was not allowed to take an oath. A similar taboo was laid upon a priestess of Athena, at Athens.[2]

<hr>

[1] Sallust, *Catil.* 51. *Isaiah*, xxxviii. 18. Suet. *Julius*, 13. D'Aubigné, *Hist. Ref.* i. c. 3.

Naples and Garibaldi, 311. Plut. *R. Q.* 44.

There is a familiar proverb, "Talk of the devil, and he will appear." This carries us back to a superstition, that the presence of a spirit could be ensured by naming it. The list of names possessed by the pontiffs in their *indigitamenta* was thus a most efficacious magical instrument, laying at their mercy all the forces of the spirit world. There was a special reason against invoking lightly the name of Jupiter. The appearance of the god, the thunderer, was so terrible that he must be invoked only in the ways approved by him. According to the old story, when Jove appeared, King Numa fell down as if dead. It was wrong for a man even to know the arts whereby the god could be drawn down to earth.[1]

Not only can the presence of a god be ensured by the use of certain words; material things can also be gained. When a Zulu sneezes, and is thus for the moment in close relation with a spirit, it is enough for him to mention what he wants, and thus the words, "a cow," "children," are prayers. This is like the modern superstition about wishing at the first sight of the new moon. The wishes are really prayers. So, too, when the Italian peasant danced round the altar of Ceres, his cry of " Ceres," or " corn, was as much a prayer as the shouts, "Give us a good vintage," "Give us a good harvest." The magical virtues attributed to prayer gave rise to the rule that all supplications should be made with a loud voice.

[1] Ovid, *Fasti*, iii. 325.

"So speak to God," says Seneca, "as though all men heard your prayers." The chasm that parts ancient from modern ideas is nowhere more broad than in the use of prayer as a means to satisfying the worst desires. "How many are the prayers which a man is ashamed to confess to himself; how few which we can make in the presence of a listener. The wicked man propitiates heaven by the gift of a boar or an ox. Aloud he says, 'Father Janus,' or 'Apollo.' But he whispers, 'Grant, O fair Laverna' (a goddess who superintended roguery) 'that I may take men in, and may seem just and holy. Spread night over my sins, and cast a cloud over my deceit.'"[1]

Sometimes the utterance of a wish had the magical power necessary to ensure its fulfilment. At other times the prayer was accompanied by offerings, as though, by itself, it had insufficient spiritual momentum to reach its goal. In so far as sacrifice was a means of ensuring the presence and countenance of a deity, it was adopted naturally when prayer was to be made. If the frugal country housewife cannot afford to give a costly victim, she must appease, with crackling salt and sacred meal, the Penates who have turned away their faces. Only when Aeneas has sacrificed seven oxen and seven sheep, does he make his supplication to Phoebus. As in offering a victim, so in praying, which is only a special mode of

<hr>

[1] Tylor, *Prim. Cult.* ii. 367. Virg. *Georg.* i. 347. Sen. *Ep.* 10. Hor. *Ep.* i. 16, 58.

sacrifice, a gift accompanied by words, the worshipper stands with his head veiled.[1]

Since prayer could be made best at the appointed shrine of a deity—where his presence had already been manifested—his temple was opened as a favour and a boon to the worshippers. On entering the temple, the Roman kissed his hand to the image, turned completely round, and prostrated himself. He then touched the altar, and threw a few grains of incense upon the flames. If his prayer was to the gods above, he raised his hands with the palms upwards; if to the gods below, he turned them downwards. When prayer was made to the Earth, the worshipper touched the ground. After the great victory which brought the second Punic war to a close, the city praetor ordained that the sacristans should throw open all the sanctuaries throughout the city, in order that, for a whole day, the people might have an opportunity of visiting and blessing the gods and rendering thanks.[2]

A certain sanctity seems to attach to the knees. The Jews regarded them as the special seat of a man's strength. The feet and knees of the gods were touched and handled in prayer, " perhaps," says Pliny, " because they are the seat of life." The suppliant, in like manner, knelt and embraced the

---

[1] Hor. *Carm.* iii. 23, 17.   Virg. *Aen.* vi. 56.

[2] Lucr. v. 1198.   The worshipper turned *dextrorsum*)(withershins. Suet. *Vit.* 2.   Macr. *Sat.* iii. 9, 1.   Virg. *Aen.* iv. 205).   Liv. xxx. 17.

knees of the man to whom he made his request. The kneeling attitude of the worshipper brought him in contact with the earth of the holy place. It is a kind of prostration, and probably took its rise in the worship of Earth, and was then extended to other worships. The story of Antaeus gives us a useful hint; the prostrate devotee renews his strength by contact with the ground. After his fourfold triumph, Julius Caesar ascended on his knees the steps of the Capitol. So the sacred stairs near St. John Lateran are still ascended. The Mahometan, during his prayers, drops upon his knees, places his hands upon the ground a little before his knees, and puts his nose and forehead also to the ground, the former first between his two hands. In time of pestilence the Roman matrons threw themselves on the temple pavements, and swept them with their loosened hair. This act is capable of being interpreted like kneeling.[1]

The vow was a peculiar kind of prayer. The worshipper promised certain offerings, provided that the prayers, which accompanied the promise, were realised. In this way he ensured that his gifts should not fail of their effect. In no respect is the business-like temper of Roman worship more obvious than here. The conditions of the vow were recorded upon wax tablets, and sealed as a kind of contract. If the god failed to perform his part, the worshipper

[1] Plin. *N. H* xi. 250. Arnob. vi. 16. Dio Cass. xliii. 21. Liv. iii. 7.

was free from his vow. On the other hand, the worshipper was bound to carry out his promises, if his prayers were answered. The tablets were hung upon the knees of the god, so that he might be reminded of them continually. Vows were made conditional upon recovery from disease, upon safe return from a journey, upon victory over an enemy, and many other occasions. A servant of the pontiffs had suffered from weak eyes, and had been given up by the physicians. But he vowed a white heifer to the Good Goddess, and he records with delight that he was cured by her, and fulfilled his vow. Often the cure was acknowledged by the gift of a gold, or silver, or earthen representation of the part healed. The Romans suffered severely from weak eyes, and from gout ; hence the eyes, the hands, and the feet, that were hung in grateful acknowledgment upon the temple walls at Nemi. In one example, there is a clay figure with the abdomen cut open to display the viscera. Every year the Brethren of the Field fulfilled the vows made the previous year for the emperor's safety, and formed new ones that he might be kept alive and victorious for another year. Pliny writes to Trajan that he prays the gods to permit him, along with the whole state, to fulfil the old vow, and perform the new one. Horace sets aside a heifer to be sacrificed in the event of his friend's return.[1]

[1] Wilm. *Inss.* 71. Classical Coll. Castle Museum, Nottingham, No. 131. Hor. *Ep.* i. 3, 36.

The gifts of like for like, in cases of disease, suggest that the life of the animal was vowed as an equivalent of the life of the man who went into a foreign country. The returning Roman was thought to be like one snatched from the gods of the strange land. Hence the man who saved a citizen's life in battle, was guarded, by a magical wreath, from the wrath of the spirits whom he had despoiled of the life due to them. When the Roman returned home, he sent word to his wife, in order that she might take the proper precautions. What these may have been is uncertain. If we may judge by parallels in folklore, the first life on which he set eyes was devoted instead of the wanderer himself; hence his wife would avoid being the first to meet him. In the story of Nicht Nought Nothing, the king has to cross a great river on his return, and the giant who carries him stipulates that he shall have the king's son as payment. The wise woman made Childe Lambton swear that he would put to death the first thing that met him as he crossed the threshold of Lambton Hall, if he were fortunate enough to kill the worm. So Jethro vowed that he would sacrifice, by fire, whosoever came out of his house to meet him, and although his only daughter came, he fulfilled his vow. A more primitive idea than that of substitution may have lain at the foundation of this usage. The blood shed on the return retied the communal bond.[1]

[1] Jacobs, *More English Fairy Tales*, 201. Lang, *Custom and Myth*, ' A Far-travelled Tale." *Judges*, xi. 31.

Let us pass now from the prayers of the Roman, to the music and dancing which also formed an integral part of his worship. The origin of music seems to have been in the loud noises by which evil spirits were driven away. This would be fitly done at the commencement of the year's work. On Plough Monday, in the neighbourhood of Nottingham, bands of men, "plough bullocks," as they are called, are led by a "Bessy"—a man bedizened as an old woman—and there is much blowing of horns by his companions. The use of the disguise looks like an attempt to deceive the evil spirits. So at Rome, the fluteplayers used to go round the city on January 13, dressed in women's clothes. The music, therefore, which accompanied sacrifice, has apparently a magical efficacy.[1]

It was the same with dancing. In the villages of Devonshire, on the eve of Twelfth-day, the farmer takes a pitcher of cider, and goes to the orchard, attended by his workmen. They encircle a tree, and drink a toast three times. They believe that if they neglect this custom, the trees will bear no apples during the year. A like magic must be employed to produce the Easter fire at Jerusalem. "It seems to be the belief of the Arab Greeks that unless they run round the sepulchre a certain number of times the fire will not come." English children, as they dance in a ring, singing "Here we go round the

[1] Plut. *R. Q.* 55.

mulberry bush," are enacting a religious rite, which is still thought by many people to have much efficacy. So at Rome the dancers, *salii*, danced in a solemn triple measure round the altars. Now they moved together, now in turn, singing the ancient Hymn of the Dancers. They were of two colleges, one of the Palatine, the other of the Quirinal. They numbered twelve in each college, and were chosen by co-optation from the noblest families in Rome. They had a master, a *premier danseur* or *praesul*, and a choirmaster, *vates*. Appius Claudius, a man who had enjoyed the honours of a triumph, was a member of the College of Dancers, and prided himself on being a better performer than his colleagues. Throughout the sacred month of Mars, they took part in the festivals; moved through the city in solemn step with singing, or danced round the altars of the gods. The ancient shrine of Mars in the Regia was open, and they took down from the walls the sacred shields, which, in the silence of the night, clashed together mysteriously. The sacrifices in which they took part were followed by banquets, the luxury of which, as of the feasts provided by St. Julian for his votaries, passed into a proverb.[1]

One of the most important Roman rites—the sacrifice of the October Horse—followed immediately upon chariot races in the Field of Mars. The right

---

[1] *Book of Days*, i. 86. *Life of Dean Stanley*, i. 458. Dion. H. *Antiq. Rom.* ii. 70. Dio C. xliv. 17. Macr. *Sat.* iii. 14, 14.

hand horse of the victorious team was sacrificed to Mars. At the same time the tail of the animal was cut off, and carried, still dripping with blood, to the altar of the Regia. The head of the horse was fought for by the inhabitants of the *Via Sacra* and of the *Suburra*. If the men of the *Via Sacra* were the conquerors, they fixed the head upon the king's palace on the Palatine hill; while if the victory fell to the men of the Suburra, the head was fixed upon the Mamilian tower. The purpose of the sacrifice was said to be for the success of the harvest, *ob frugum eventum*. Like the horse brought out on midsummer night in King's County, it seems also to have represented all cattle. Its blood was kept in the temple of Vesta until the succeeding spring. It was then mixed with some beanstalks, and with the blood of the calf sacrificed to Mother Earth, for use in the spring purifications of the Parilia. In some parts of Germany, St. Stephen's day is called "the great horse day." The horses are raced round the fields until they sweat abundantly. They are taken then to the blacksmith, who bleeds them that they may remain sound throughout the year. Their blood is kept as a cure for various ailments. Both the Roman and the German festival are characterized by the magical meaning which belongs to primitive ritual. At a later stage of development the races are thought to be held in honour of some god.[1]

[1] Preller, *R.M.* I³. 366, 416. Plut. *R.Q.* 97. Mannhardt, *A.F.W.* i. 403.

A sacred character attached also to the games that were held in the hollow between the Palatine and Aventine Hills. At first the great circus was only "a field where they play," adjoining the altar of Consus, a god of farming. The altar lay at the south-east corner of the Palatine Hill, and was buried in the earth. Judging from analogies, it seems to have been one of those fetish stones of which traces are not infrequent in Roman religion. It was brought out only on the twenty-first of August. The festival of Consus was celebrated again on the fifteenth of December. The first celebration came when the harvest was over—the latter, when all the corn, fruit, and wine of the year were stored away. At these feasts the horses and asses enjoyed a respite from their work, and were wreathed with garlands. All the citizens resorted to the August festival. Each of the thirty wards or *curiae* had its appointed ground, and the custom arose of erecting stands of wood from which to view the show. The sacred character was not lost until a late date. "Of old," sings Ovid, "the country folk came into the city to the games; but that service was done to the gods, and not for pleasure's sake."[1]

There was an ancient legend that the Sabine women were carried off at this festival. This suggests that part of the ceremonial consisted in foot races, in which some detail gave rise to the

[1] Liv. i. 35. Plut. *R. Q.* 48. Ovid, *Fasti*, iii. 783.

story. This may, indeed, have been the first stage ; for foot races often pass into horse races.[2]

Let us now pass to the games, as they were carried out in historical times. We have seen that place is made for the thirty curiae, in order that all Rome may be there to witness. Much more must place be made for the gods of Rome. The images were brought in all their solemn attire down from the Capitol, on cars of ivory and silver. By their side walked the companies of the priests and the sacred colleges. The most prominent figure, however, was the chief magistrate, who led the way, standing on a high chariot drawn by white horses. He was attired in the tunic of Jove, and wore from his shoulders a toga of Tyrian purple, embroidered with palm leaves of gold. A laurel wreath was on his head, and a slave, standing in the same chariot, held above him a crown of oak leaves, made of jewels and gold. An ivory sceptre was in his hand, surmounted by an eagle. These insignia were brought from their resting-place in the temple of Jove, to whom they were sacred. For the magistrate was to be the earthly embodiment of the god presiding at the festival of his people. The friends and clients of the presiding magistrate took their places on either side of his chariot, and with him led the way from the hill along the forum, the *vicus Tuscus*, and the cattle market, and swept through the centre gate

---

[1] Mannhardt, *A. F. W.* i. 383.

of the circus into the vast open space, to the music of horn-blowers, harpers, and pipers. As they made a circuit of the arena, the people arose and clapped their hands; invoking the gods, who were taken from their cars, and put on the sacred couch in order to view the sports. But the absorbing interest of the races that followed made the spectators impatient with this preliminary ceremonial. It was this circumstance, doubtless, that led Ovid to contrast the pious temper of antiquity with the impatience that resented any obstacle to its satisfaction.[1]

It is clear, then, that ancient ritual was very complex, and that sacrifice included much more than the slaughter of a living creature. We are prepared now to pass to this important part of the whole function, without overlooking the contributions made to it by word or gesture; the prayers, music, and dancing.

The natural development of Roman ideas of sacrifice, in the special sense of offering a victim, was interrupted by the introduction of Etruscan and Greek usages. Only here and there can we light upon what is original. Elaborate ordinances, indeed, were laid down by the pontiffs and haruspices, in which the kinds of victims to be sacrificed to the several deities were recounted; whether they were to be young or full grown, male or female. According to these rules, again, oxen were to be offered to Jove

---

[1] Mayor's n. on Juv. x. 36 ff.

Neptune, Mars, or Apollo; swine to Juno, Ceres, Bona Dea, Silvanus. It is seldom, however, that we can find a genuine Roman ceremony.[1]

A few rites have the character of being original, and furnish clues to primitive ideas of sacrifice. On the fifteenth of April a cow in calf was offered by the pontiffs, at the temple on the Capitoline Hill; and like offerings were made at the thirty curiae. This mode of sacrifice seems to have come down from a remote antiquity. Similar sacrifices were made by the Greeks to the Eumenides. At Rome, the unborn young were taken and burnt by the senior vestal, and the ashes were kept for use at the city festival of Pales.[2]

Two things are obvious in these rites of the *fordicidia*; namely, that the burning of the victim is a kind of fire charm, and that the ashes have a magical efficacy. We must take account here of the sacredness of fire. The burning of the victim brings it under a magical influence. For it is hardly possible to regard the act of burning merely as a means of disposing of the flesh, so that it may not be exposed to casual contact. This is emphasised further by the participation of the fire-maidens in the rite. This aspect of burnt offerings is prominent in some customs, where the sacrifice consists in burning, and nothing more. On midsummer night the Parisians used to put cages or sacks of cats,

[1] Cic. *Div.* ii. 29.   [2] Pausan. II. ii. 4.

as many as two dozen at a time, and sometimes foxes, over the flames; and the bystanders thought it of good omen when the cries of the dying animals were piercing. They were hung, in a basket, on a mast raised near the Hôtel de Ville, in the Place de Grêve. In Metz there used to be a bonfire on the Esplanade, in which six cats were burnt along with the fuel. So at Rome, on the last day of the games held in honour of Ceres, there was a fox hunt in the circus, torches being tied to the animals' tails. From the sacred character of fire two results seem to follow. On the one hand, the victim is devoured by the fire, and thus sustains the magical element. Although few traces remain of this belief, there is little doubt that the fire was viewed as a spirit that could be so nourished. Vesta, says Ovid, is the living flame. On the other hand, the victim at the *fordicidia* is cleansed, and its substance receives power by the fire, so that the ashes convey its virtues, purified and undiminished, to the flame through which the citizens leap at the feast of Pales. Roman sacrifice is thus a magical rite, not only through the words and gestures employed, but also as regards the victim slain. We find this in the ceremony of the October horse. The use of its blood in the lustral bonfire, and of its tail as an aspergill, communicated its properties, through contact, to the citizens who were present at the ceremony of lustration. The same efficacy attached to the bodies of sacred persons.

The dust of ancestors made the home round which, in early times, they were buried, sacred indeed. Still more must this have been the case with the human victims slaughtered for the welfare of the community. For the power of such rites was intrinsic at first, and did not depend, in the primitive idea, upon the will of the deity to whom they were celebrated. The Hindus believe, indeed, that sacrifice can be used as a means to extort from the gods whatever is desired. So the Romans believed that Jupiter could be drawn down from heaven, not of his own will, but in conformity with the wishes of his worshipper. The power of ritual stands over against the power of the god, and is not derived from it.[1]

How is it that the flesh of the victim is credited with these marvellous powers ? The answer to this question, as to nearly every other relating to folklore, is a complex one. A striking coincidence, or some touch of that awe of Nature which culminates in Nature-worship, may attract attention to any part of the living world, and when any creature has been thus marked out, the religious imagination explains the fact now in one way, now in another. Let us suppose, then, that a tribe of men unite in ascribing a sacred character to some animal. They may have reached this point along any of the paths of primitive reasoning. When they begin to reflect, in

---

[1] Mannhardt, *A. F. IV.* i. 515. Ovid, *Fasti*, vi. 291. M. Williams, *Hinduism*, 40.

the pictorial manner of savages, they will very naturally explain the protection afforded to them by the victim, or the powers exercised by it, through a relation between the sacred being and the tribe. It is their kinsman, their father, mother, or brother. This process of savage thought is almost universal in its prevalence.   Without expecting that it will take precisely the same form everywhere, we may interpret the sanctity of the victim as involving a kind of kinship to the tribe.   Here, once more, we find a logical consequence of that primitive idea of holiness, which makes it to depend upon the communal interests.   Nor does it seem necessary to treat this sanctity of an animal as bound up with a particular etiquette of marriage.   The belief in the kinship of the sacred animal may coexist with diverse marriage customs.

Beliefs of this kind must differ in the case of wild animals, on the one hand, and domesticated cattle on the other.   The feeling of relationship must have taken a special form in so far as the milk of cows and goats was used for food.   The Italians viewed with reverence both kinds of creature.   In this they differed from the Jews, whose sacrifices were confined to domestic animals, and who regarded other sacrifices as unclean.

There are some interesting evidences which go to prove that the Italians considered themselves to have a certain kinship with their sacred animals.

Plutarch wants to know why a wisp of hay used to be tied to the horns of savage cattle. This is, perhaps, a survival from the time when all cattle were sacred to the god Mars. The wisp of hay was the token of this, just as it showed that the soldiers who marched under the manipular standard were the men of Mars. There was an old legend to the effect that the Sabines, once upon a time, were hard pressed by the Umbrians, and that they vowed a *holy spring*, that is to send beyond their borders, the sons and daughters who were born in the year of war. One band, led by the ox of Mars, came down into the centre of Italy. A like account is given of the Picentes or woodpecker people, who were led by the sacred bird into the marches of Ancona, and the Hirpini, or wolves, who were led into the region of Beneventum. The wolf festival at Rome, and the wolfish gestures of those who took part in it, show that the Romans believed in some special bond which united the life of the animal and that of the citizens. This feeling found voice, too, in the old story of the suckling of Romulus and Remus. During the Social War, the Samnites issued a denarius, the obverse of which was stamped with a bull trampling upon a wolf. This is manifestly an allegory of the conflict between Samnium and Rome. According to Pliny, the Roman armies used to have for standards not wolves only, but eagles, man-bulls, horses, and boars. Light is shed upon the slaughter of the October horse, when it appears that the horse figured as an ancient ensign. The sacred boar is doubtless represented in sacrifice by the offering of swine, and by the name of the second month in the year, *Aprilis* or Boar month. The belief in sacred animals akin to man, prepares the way for the idea of transmigration as found in India, or of metamorphosis as in Greece; at Rome the superstition that witches passed into wolves may have originated in ancient rites like those of Soracte.[1]

Why should the sacred animal be killed? The answer has already been given in the case of burnt offerings. The life taken is communicated to the sacred flame. When the victim is eaten, instead of being burnt, the morsels of the magical body act as talismans for those who join in the festival. Here the act of killing is, so to speak, incidental to the use of the victim for a religious purpose. When, however, the primitive view of sacrifice as a magical rite is taken up into the outlook of a more developed imagination, the meaning of the whole function is found in the taking of life. Trebatius, indeed, marks this off as one of two main kinds of sacrifice: "There is one," he says, "in which the will of the gods is enquired through inspection of the entrails, the other is that in which the life only is devoted to the deity." We do not find, however, that either of these explana-

---

[1] Plut. *R. Q.* 71. Mommsen, *R. H.* i. 123. Baumeister, *Denkm.* 1178. Pliny, *N. H.* x. 16.

tions is fitted to account for the rites we have just been considering.[1]

At the same time, Trebatius' second division points us to the idea which underlay the later form of sacrifice as a common meal. The life of the community was renewed in the life of the victim. Here, also, we are able to study a custom in a genuine Italian festival. The great celebration on the Alban Mount which the consuls used to hold, before setting out for their province, was dependent for its efficacy upon the participation of all the townships that united in it. It was necessary that some one should come from each city to share in the flesh of the victims. In like manner, open house was kept at Rome by all the wealthier classes during the great thanksgiving feasts. The success of the ritual was dependent, in some measure, upon the number of those who shared in it. "The law of the feast was open-handed hospitality: the sacrifice was not complete without guests." When Ezra read the book of the law, after the return from captivity, there was a public feast, to which all had access, and portions were sent to those who, otherwise, would have remained without a share in the festival. The rule that all must partake may have gained force from the religious formalism of the Roman. If an accustomed place was vacant, there was a danger lest the change, slight in itself, should vitiate the

<hr>

[1] Macr. *Sat.* iii. 5, 1.

whole proceedings. When the god came to be distinguished from the victim, he used to be present at the common meal of his people; and so all the community was gathered together.[1]

We find, then, side by side, rites such as those of the October Horse, in which the reference to the spirit worshipped is very obscure, and other rites—such as most ceremonial sacrifices—in which the reference in question is quite clear. The distinction between the two is found also when we pass to the offering of first fruits. We have seen that great importance attached to the beginnings of things; the first word spoken, the first thing seen or heard. Hence it becomes advisable to inaugurate each important season of the year, and each time of life, by auspicious words and acts. Just as the new year and the birthday must begin with good omens, so is it with the harvest both of corn and of wine. The solemn festival of the Brethren of the Field was especially one of first-fruits. The citizen did not even taste of the new corn and wine until the priests had eaten and drunk of them. Numa, it was said, ordained that the corn should be baked; and forbade the employment of any other in ritual. The reason given by Pliny states that corn is more wholesome when it is cooked. It is possible, however, that we are dealing here with traces of a fire charm. When these same acts are looked at by devotees of more imagination, they are interpreted

<hr>

[1] *Rel. Sem.* 236. *Nehem.* viii. 12.

by reference to the will of the harvest spirit. The magical beginning of the harvest appears then to be an offering of first fruits to a deity.[1]

"In some places," says Varro, "the beginning of the vintage is made publicly by the priests; and this is the case at Rome. For the Flamen Dialis commences the vintage. When the time comes to pluck the grapes, he sacrifices a lamb to Jupiter, and begins between the killing of the lamb, and the offering of its flesh." In like manner the ritual law of Tusculum forbade the sale of wine, until the priest had proclaimed the festival of opening the casks.[2]

It seems reasonable to suppose that the festival of first-fruits reaches back into those primitive times when there was, as yet, no settled pantheon. The labourer in an English harvest field who pours on the ground the first drops of his ale, in order (he explains) that it may run clear, is repeating an act familiar to the Romans. Yet it is possible that the long list of his predecessors may never have gone beyond the belief in the simple efficacy of the rite. They may never have thought that the libation pleased any spirit—whether of the field or of the corn. We must look elsewhere for the origin of this belief. The idea that the spirits need food is very manifest in the offerings which the Romans made to their dead; and this belief had some effect, doubtless,

---

[1] Pliny, *N. H.* xviii. 2.

[2] Varro, *L. L.* vi. 16. Mommsen, *R. H.* i. 196.

upon their interpretation of other traditional usages. In India, the gods are supposed to need their food. By sacrifice, says the Vishnu Purana, the gods are nourished. In the offering of first-fruits, therefore, we have an act performed first for its magical efficacy, and subsequently regarded as part of the service of a spirit.[1]

Just as the gods of Rome joined in the sacred games, so they were thought to be present at the sacred banquet. The quaint simplicity of Roman ideas about religion is nowhere more striking than here. The sacred banquets were held originally in thanksgiving, and, by an innovation, as an expedient to avert pestilence. Couches were set in the open spaces. These were spread with the most costly coverlets and cushions, and the images of the gods were placed upon them. Tables were brought, and a sumptuous meal was laid out. When the banquet had been eaten symbolically by the gods, it was handed over to the College of the Feasters, *septem-viri epulones*. On two occasions during Cæsar's campaigns in Gaul, the Senate commanded that thanksgivings should be held for three weeks. Throughout this time every house in the city was thrown open, and all were welcomed to the citizens' tables. Private enmities were suspended. The law courts were closed. Prisoners were set free from their chains.[2]

[1] M. Williams, *Hinduism*, 39.
[2] Caesar, *B. G.* iv. 38 ; vii. 90.

We have thus traced the development of Roman sacrifice, from its magical form to that stage in which it is viewed as a communion with the god. The most powerful factor in this process seems to have been the employment of images. They secured the presence of the god, in the same way as the images made by the witches secured the presence of their victims. The image is a magical object, and brings the god to the assembly of his worshippers. In the absence of the god, his benefits could not be counted upon. Only at a later stage of religious thought is the divine will regarded as adequate in itself to operate apart from these physical means. In particular, the look of the god was believed to protect. As the worshippers filled the temple, they were all under the guardianship of the solemn figure whose countenance was turned upon them, "raining influence." When some Indians set out on an expedition across Lake Superior, the chief, in a very loud voice, addressed a prayer to the Great Spirit, entreating him to give them a good look to cross the lake.[1]

At one of the sacred banquets there was a dreadful omen. The images of the gods turned their faces from the feast that was laid before them. This is explained when Livy tells us, that the mice got to the olives before the dinner began, and that the dish which was set before Jove fell off the table, covers and all. When the gods are thus averse, that is

[1] Tylor, *P. C.* ii. 366.

when they have turned away their faces, special means must be taken to regain their favour. In this particular case the Roman games were repeated.[1]

Just as the god's presence was secured by determinate rites, so, if he seemed to delay his coming, the same rites were used with more earnestness, or older ones were revived. As the meaning of ritual was lost, its use tended to be interrupted. Only when the presence of some calamity roused the dormant religious sense was the ancient ceremonial practised, with the old seriousness, though with an imperfect consciousness of its original meaning. Thus the human sacrifices which, in all probability, formed once a considerable part of the sacrificial ritual of Rome, were revived on rare occasions, as when the two Greeks and the two Gauls were buried alive. So, too, the old meaning of lustration being lost, the water and the fire are used not as a regular means of securing strength and freedom from disease, but to drive away some special evil which has alarmed the devotee.[2]

When the advance of knowledge made it impossible to adhere any longer to the literal interpretations of primitive uses, they were replaced by allegorical ones. The material facts were treated as representative of moral conditions. The notion of physical weakness to be done away by the magical offices

[1] Liv. xl. 59.   [2] Plut. *R. Q.* 83.

of religion, passes into the notion of ceremonial guilt, and thereby to the notion of moral guilt, when religion is viewed in the light of adoration paid to moral beings. At this stage the priest passes from the primitive medicine man to the spiritual consoler. " Let him free from fear," says one, "the transgressor who has expiated his fault." The water of sprinkling and of baptism was thought to have the power in itself of removing the stains of crime. The sense of protection which ancient ritual thus gave was reflected in a certain carelessness of temper. Even Ovid finds his countrymen too light-hearted in this respect. When Pilate took water, and washed his hands from the innocent blood of Jesus, he showed himself to be one with those to whom the poet addressed his rebuke a generation before : " Ah, too light of heart are ye who think that the stern accusations of murder can be done away in the water of a river."[1]

Not only were spiritual meanings read into ancient ritual by more enlightened ages. The more savage elements in it were discarded. In Ovid's time it began to be believed that the earliest sacrifices were bloodless. The new Pythagoreans, in particular, attacked the customs of animal sacrifice. In India, animals are now sacrificed only to Kali.

In the same spirit, later theologians explained the sacrifice of animals by reference to substitution.

[1] Ovid, *Fasti*, ii. 45.

The notion of a life kindred with that of mankind accounts for the interchange of human and animal sacrifices. Yet it is not necessary to assume that at first sacrifice was performed always with human victims. The flesh of the kindred boar, or horse, or ox, was as effective a talisman as that of the human being. The belief that the life of the man or animal was bound up with certain parts of the body, was another factor by which ancient usages must have been affected. The time when the priests of Jove and Vesta ceased to be sacrificed, may date from the burial of their hair under the sacred trees. The story of the charm against thunder, therefore, may have a basis in fact. The man's hair may have been given for his life.

Roman worship culminated in the ceremonial of sacrifice ; in it all the ideas we have been considering found expression. Let us suppose ourselves transported across the centuries into an Italian town of Ovid's time, and to wake on the morning of a holy day.[1] The day of sacrifice must be of good omen. If it prove inauspicious, the sacred duty, unless appointed specially for the occasion, will be put off. The first favourable moment must be seized. In order that no evil influence may be aroused by an idle expression, those who are to take part in the ceremony choose carefully words of good omen, or

---

[1] *Note.* The description that follows has been combined from many sources, and is not representative of any single ceremonial.

even keep a religious silence. Ovid, by a later refinement, enjoins on the worshipper to cultivate a good intention. Serenity and joyousness of countence and bearing were a duty. There was neither mourner nor sign of mourner to be seen. Every word of lamentation was left unspoken. The mourner was thought to be polluted by the death of his kinsman, and was excluded from the public ceremonies. So, too, at Jerusalem, "the Levites stilled all the people, saying, Hold your peace, for the day is holy, neither be ye grieved." The same festal mood was cultivated by the citizens in their dwellings. "What am I to do on the holy day of Neptune?" Horace asks, and then he bids the singing-girl bring out the old Caecuban wine, that they may drink together, and chant the praises of Neptune and Diana. The costume of the citizens bore witness to the sacred season. The toga was sent to the fuller, that it might be made white for the holiday. The concourse of the worshippers thus attired dazzled the eye under the bright Italian sun, and seemed to melt into the white stucco or marble of the streets and public edifices. Moreover, work was abstained from, lest any casual act should render fruitless the ceremonies of the day. The king of worship and the flamens were not allowed to see work done at sacred seasons, and announced this by the crier. It was only permitted to the citizens to do that of which the omission would cause harm.

"The sanctity of the day," Scaevola said, in the spirit of the Jewish doctors, "was not broken if a man dragged an ox out of a pit." The Roman holy days, therefore, were kept as strictly as Sunday in Protestant countries. There was a distinction drawn in this respect. The times when the *mundus* was open, the Saturnalia, and the Latin Festival were kept most strictly. The private feast of purification after a death, *feriae denicales*, was also one of great solemnity. Other occasions, public or private, were observed with more freedom. In the country, seven days were given to work, and on the eighth the countryman came to town, to attend the market, and to perform his religious duties. In the interest of the farmer it was decided that the law courts could be open on the market day.[1]

The lot of the slave and the artisan was lightened considerably by the numerous holidays. The man of higher station welcomed his freedom from public business. It was in moments snatched thus from politics that Cicero pursued his literary and philosophical studies. The number of holidays, however, became so great as to be a public inconvenience. Augustus diminished them by thirty. Two centuries later Marcus Aurelius fixed one hundred and thirty-five days as the limit.[2]

---

[1] Liv. i. 45. Ovid, *Fasti*, i. 71. *Nehemiah*, viii. 11. Hor. *Carm.* iii. 28. Plut. *Numa*, 14. Macr. *Sat.* i. 16. Dio Cass. *fr.* 25.

[2] Suet. *Aug* 32.

At the early morning hour appointed for the sacrifice, the precincts of the temples are crowded with worshippers. Chaplets are set upon the heads of the gods, and their images are anointed. The altars which stand before them in the temples are wreathed with vervain, that is, with the green leaves of sacred trees, such as laurel, olive, and myrtle. Saffron and laurel are burnt with the incense, in order that the crackling of the flames may furnish a good omen. The shimmer of the altar fires is reflected from the many polished surfaces of marble and of metal, and especially from the gilt compartments of the ceilings. The shining pavements within, and the paths without, are strewn with "violets," that is, with wallflowers and stocks.[1]

The slaughter of the sacred victims is to take place at the great altar outside the temple, perhaps a round structure like that which stood upon a foundation of several steps at the north-east corner of the temple of Diana at Nemi. The white bulls, with their horns gilt, and the white sheep, brought for sacrifice from the famous pastures of Clitumnus, are scared and restive under the glances of the throng. And now the chosen victims are led away, in order that the sacred procession may be formed. The magistrate who is to conduct the sacrifice has washed his hands in water from a living stream.

[1] Macr. *Sat.* iii. 13, 8. Ovid, *Fasti*, i. 76, 344. Mayor's n. Juv. xii. 90.

He has girt up his toga in the ancient manner of Gabii, taking one of the loose ends and twisting it round his waist. He is also veiled in part by raising over the back of the head that fold of the toga which passes round the shoulders. The attendants who follow are also wreathed with chaplets of leaves and flowers, or fillets of sacred wool. The fire on the altar has been brought in a brazier from some pure source, perhaps from the sacred hearth of Vesta herself. Religious silence is proclaimed to all the bystanders, and they are sprinkled with holy water by means of an aspergill, perhaps a horse's tail. The flute-player shrills forth a strain from his pipes of ivory. As the magistrate comes near the altar, one reads to him the set form of words from an ancient book of ritual, and he, turning to the east, repeats them carefully, lest a word misplaced or misspoken should render the rite fruitless. He then takes incense from the casket offered to him, and new wine, unmixed with water, from a flat golden bowl which is handed to him by the *camillus*, a boy of noble descent, whose father and mother are still living. The incense is scattered, and the wine poured over the flames. Then a victim is led up. Its head is sprinkled with meal and salt, and a few hairs are cut off and thrown into the fire. It was of great importance that it should seem to come willingly, and a few grains of corn or drops of water were let fall into its ears, that it might shake its head, and seem to nod assent to the sacrifice. Two men slay the animal; one of them stuns it with a maul, while the other brings the sacred knife, which has been sprinkled with salt and grain. The latter asks the magistrate for his order to kill, and he replies, THIS DO, *hoc age.* The permission being given, he cuts its throat. A basin is held under the wound, and the blood which flows is handed to the celebrant, who pours it upon the altar. He wipes his hands upon a cloth of rough texture, the use of which is kept up in the ornamental band or scarf which priests of the Roman Church wear upon the left arm. The animal is now prepared for food. The skull is either burnt upon the altar, or hung upon the temple wall, in order to be a token of the sacrifice. Of its entrails, the heart, the lungs, and the liver were set aside upon a charger, to be committed later to the flames. When the victims were killed in order to ascertain the will of the gods, the entrails were examined carefully, and if they were favourable, the rite had been successfully accomplished. In the year 208 B.C. victims were offered for some days without success, *sine litatione,* and the peace of the gods was not gained. There was an interval between the sacrifice and the offering of the entrails. This might be brief, or else it lasted from the morning until the evening. The sacred silence was suspended in the meantime, and was renewed when the entrails were burnt.[1]

[1] Liv. xxvii. 23. Wilm. 2879.

With the shedding of the blood upon the altar the religious part of the ceremonial culminated. The rest of the feast, though indeed sacred, was passed in the feeling that all was well between man and heaven. The flesh was roasted upon spits of hazel or willow. Bread was brought upon trays, and wine was served. During the banquet hymns were raised to the god of the feast, by men who moved in solemn measure round the altars. This part of the ceremony took its rise in the shouts by which the worshipper summoned the god to the feast, and was the fore-runner of the prayers and hymns, which have come to be the chief part of modern worship. Horace was one of the first, among the Romans, to give poetic expression to these utterances. His most famous sacred poem was the Secular Hymn, which he wrote at the command of Augustus, to be sung by a choir of boys and girls at the games of the year 17 B.C. His lyrics were learnt by the children of succeeding generations, and must have been often on their lips to while away the moments as they walked along the country lanes ; set perhaps to plain and strenuous music like that of the Delphic hymn.

LATIN INDEX

Abeona, 134.
Adeona, 134.
altilanei, 263.
annus, 74.
apex, 263.
Aprilis, 294.
auguraculum, 188.
auspex, 187.

Bacchanalia, 247.

camenae, 122.
casa Romuli, 237.
camillus, 306.
comitia calata, 265.
confarreatio, 264.
coniectores, 48.
curator aquarum, 181.

Deverra, 103, 134.
dies violationis, 63.
dii manes, 59, 64.
Domiduca, 134.

Educa, 134.
epulones, 298.

favissae, 235.
Favonius, 109.

feriae denicales, 304.
  ,,   Latinae, 202, 295.
Flamen Dialis, 142, 147, 164, 202,
    204, 250, 261, 297, 303.
  ,,   Martialis, 265.
  ,,   Quirinalis, 265.
flaminica, 264.
fordicidia, 289.

genius, 56.

haruspices, 192.
hirpi, 112.

indigitamenta, 104, 134, 157.
Intercidona, 103, 134.
invidia, 50.
Iterduca, 134.
iuno, 56.
iustitium, 68.

lapis manalis—
    (i) covering of *mundus*, 61.
    (ii.) rain charm, 155, 157.
lares, 243.
lemuria, 67.
litatio, 307.
lituus, 188.
Lupercalia, 108, 144, 163.
lymphatus, 125.

mathematici, 197.
Mellonia, 134.
mos maiorum, 66, 138.
mundus, 304.

orbis, 74.
oscines, 184.

parcipromus, 57.
parentare, 69.
Parilia, 58.
pax deum, 76.
persona, 16.
Pilumnus, 103, 134.
pomoerium, 188, 194.
pons sublicius, 164.
postliminium, 213.
Potina, 134.
praenomina, 249.
praepetes, 184.
praesul, 284.
psychomantia, 40.

pullarius, 13.
purus, 14.

regia, 122.
regifugium, 253, 266.
religio, 21, 213.
rex sacrorum, 139.
Robigo, 135.
Roma aeterna, 13.

sacer, 215, 259.
salii, 101, 284.
Saturnalia, 57.
Saturnus, 134.
silentium, 189.
silvanus, 102.
solanus, 113.
suggrundarium, 60.

tripudium solistimum, 189.

vates, 284.
ver sacrum, 293.

ENGLISH INDEX

Aeneid, folklore in, 41, 43.
altar, 227.
animals, behaviour of, 79.
anointing with oil, 145.
Antony, 109, 194.
Appius, friend of Cicero, 40.
Apuleius, 87.
astrology, 194.
asylum, 223.
Athenodorus, 38.
Attus Navius, 186.
augurs, 184 ff., 261.
Augustus, 25, 72, 97, 156, 193.

Baal, 218, 257.
beans, 69.
Bellona, 144.
blood, 80, 209.
burial, earth, 60.

Caesar, 241, 274, 280.
Capitoline temple, 225, 235, 240.
Carmenta, 123.
causation, 136.
Ceres, 260.
charm against thunder, 116.
Cicero, 24, 49, 51, 58, 88, 135, 144.
Clitumnus, 305.
comparative method, 129.

Consus, 286.
cornel, 100.
couvade, 245.
criminals, 259.
crow, 116.
Curtius Rufus, 33.

dancing, 283.
Decii, 256.
Descartes, 55.
divination, 174 ff.
Domitian, 36, 98.
dreams, life of, 28, interpretation of, 48.

eclipses, 195.
Egeria, 115, 121.
English law, 19, 25.
Etruscans, 165.
Evander, 123.
evil eye, 151.

father, authority of, 245.
faunus, 106 ff.
Faustulus, 115.
fire, 206 ff.
Firmanus, 196.
first fruits, 296.
flint, 164.

Fortuna Primigenia, 182.
foundations, 243.
funeral, 65, 204.
Furies, 34.

gables, 241.
gallows, 256.
games, 287.
Gods, punctilious, 47 ; genii of, 58.
government, Roman, as religious
    censor, 83, 139, 140.

head, as seat of life, 53.
heart, in divination, 192.
Hercules, 126.
Hirpini, 293.
holiness, idea of, 211.
Horace, 24, 197, 303.
— his conversion, 88.

images, 105, 230, 299.
Indian administration, 20.
insanity, 159, 161.
inspiration, 252.

Juno, 221, 225.
Jupiter, 121, 221, 225.

Khonds, 257.
king of the wood, 255.
king of worship, 139, 253, 303.
kneeling, 279.

Lang, 28.
language, effect of, 18; origin of, 21.
laurel, 98, 101.
law, Roman, 19; school of evidence,
    21.
lightning, 77, 156, 193.
liver, in divination, 192.
Livy, on marvels, 84.

lots, 180 ff.
Lucan, 16.
Lucretius, 24, 75.
lung, in divination, 192.

Maecenas, 73.
magic, 154, 161 ff.
mancipation, 148.
Marcius, 175.
Marcus, 140, 249.
Marica, 123.
Mars, driven out, 267.
Marsi, 161.
medicine, 130, 158.
metamorphosis, 152.
miracles of Vespasian, 91.
monotheism, 91.
music, 283.
mysteries, 167 ff.

Nemi, temple at, 97 ; scenery of,
    119; altar at, 230, 305; *favissa*
    at, 235 ; votive offerings a ,
    120, 281.
Nero, 36, 98.
Numa, 115, 121, 270.
numbers, 150.

October Horse, 284, 290.
Odin, 255.
oleaster, 97.
Olenus, 149.
omens, operation of, 150.
Otho, 36.
outlaw, 203.
Ovid, 24, 35, 122.
ox of Samnium, 293.

pathetic fallacy, 92.
prayer, 276.
pestilence, 132.

Picentes, 293.
Picus, 115.
Pilate, 301.
places, holy, 222.
Pliny, the Elder, 32, 154.
        the Younger, 32.
polytheism, 105.
pontiffs, 83, 273.
primitive wisdom, 130.
progress, nature of, 22.
Publicius, 175.
Pythagorean, books, 179; theories
        concerning sacrifice, 301.

rain charms, 155.
religion, Lucretius and Virgil on, 75.
Remus, 188, 243.
ritual, joyous character of, 270,
        and belief, 273.
Romulus, 100, 115, 188, 196.
round temples, 239.

sacrifice, power of, 291, surround-
        ings of, 302 ff.
Salvanel, 106.
Saturnian measure, 107.
Scaevola, 274.
Seneca, 16.
serpents, as pets, 56.
sextons, 241.
Sibyl, 176 ff.

sleep, gates of, 44.
social self, 15.
soul, primitive idea of, 55.
spinning, 147.
spiritualism, in Nottingham, 40,
        207; affinities of, with primi-
        tive religion, 130.
spoils, 146.
standards, military, 231.
Stoics, 49.
substitution, 302.
Suetonius, 32.
Summanus, 194.

taboos, power of, 202; more
        numerous in early times, ib.
Tacitus, 89, 197.
Tennyson, 42.
Terminus, 118, 162, 221, 227.
Thrasyllus, 198.
Tiberinus, 125.
Tiberius, 66, 156.
Tibullus, 24.
Trajan, 16.
Trebatius, 294.
trees, of life, 43, 99; wonderful, 79.
Twelve Tables, 164.

urn of destiny, 183.

Yggdrasil, 255.

PLYMOUTH:
WILLIAM BRENDON AND SON,
PRINTERS.

www.ingramcontent.com/pod-product-compliance
Lightning Source LLC
Chambersburg PA
CBHW031045120726
47905CB00007B/2313